Encyclopedia of Cats

A comprehensive guide to cat breeds

NorthParadePublishing

©2013 North Parade Publishing Ltd.
4 North Parade,
Bath BA11LF. UK
Printed in China.
www.nppbooks.co.uk

Contents

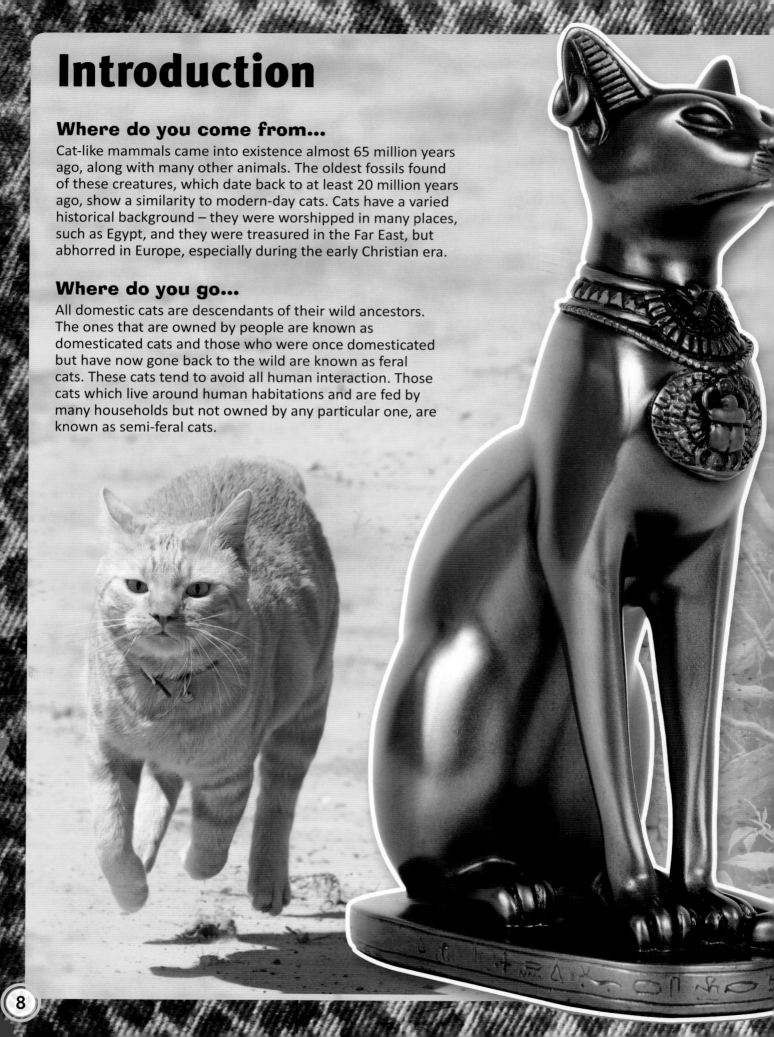

Introduction

Where do you come from...

Cat-like mammals came into existence almost 65 million years ago, along with many other animals. The oldest fossils found of these creatures, which date back to at least 20 million years ago, show a similarity to modern-day cats. Cats have a varied historical background – they were worshipped in many places, such as Egypt, and they were treasured in the Far East, but abhorred in Europe, especially during the early Christian era.

Where do you go...

All domestic cats are descendants of their wild ancestors. The ones that are owned by people are known as domesticated cats and those who were once domesticated but have now gone back to the wild are known as feral cats. These cats tend to avoid all human interaction. Those cats which live around human habitations and are fed by many households but not owned by any particular one, are known as semi-feral cats.

Come home!

Domestic cats can be pedigreed or non-pedigreed. Non-pedigreed cats are those which have not been recognised by any cat registry (such as the Cat Fanciers' Association or The International Cat Association). They are also known as 'moggies', 'mongrels' or 'mutt-cats'. Pedigreed cats, on the other hand, are those which have been recognised by these registries. Pedigreed cats can either be cross-bred (offspring of two different breeds) or purebred (offspring of parents of same breed).

The Big Fat Cat Family

The cat family is bigger than you would have thought. It comprises not only domestic cats but also big cats, such as lions, tigers, leopards, jaguars, cheetahs and many others. Most cats, with the exception of the lion, prefer to live alone. Cats generally have some pattern on their fur which helps them to stay camouflaged. The colour and pattern of their coats depends largely on their habitat.

Tiger, tiger eyes burning bright!

Of the four 'big' cats – tiger, lion, jaguar and leopard – the tiger is the largest. Reaching a length of almost 11 feet, females weigh up to 180 kg, whereas males weigh anywhere between 180 kg to 230 kg. And if you thought that was heavy, the Siberian tiger can weigh up to 320 kg! A fierce carnivorous predator, the tiger can see and hunt well in the dark too.

My lion, my pride!

Cats are solitary creatures and they like to live alone - but not the lion. Lions live in groups called a 'pride'. They even hunt in groups, but interestingly the male lions do not usually participate in hunting. It is up to the lionesses to look for prey, hunt, kill and feed the lion!

Catch me if you can!

Cheetahs, the most specialized of all cats, are the fastest land mammals in the world. Did you know they can run at a speed 90 kph? Cheetahs are often confused with leopards because both have similar patterns on their coats, but cheetahs can be identified by their characteristic 'teardrop' marks on both sides of their nose.

Living in the wild!

Did you know that all domestic cats are descended from the wildcat? Hundreds of years ago, some wildcats moved to areas inhabited by humans and started living with them. They never went back to the wild and this is how the first breed of domestic cats came about. And rest, as they say, is history.

Ocelot-ting!

Ocelots are somewhere in between a domestic and wild cat. Twice the size of a normal house cat, they are generally found in the wild, but a lot of ocelots have taken to living in a domestic set up and can be seen around villages and other human settlements. Ocelots are nocturnal predators, and they rely on their sight and hearing to hunt their prey.

Domestic Cats

The cats that we know in our day-to-day life are domestic cats. Domestic cats were not always domestic. It is believed that thousands of years ago, some cats moved out of their wild habitats and began to live in human settlements. Eventually, they started travelling with humans and this is how they spread to almost all parts of the world. The oldest evidence of the domestication of cats is in Egypt around eight thousand years ago!

The first cat!

The first cat-like animals known as Miacids roamed the Earth almost 65 million years ago. These creatures were similar to modern-day cats - so their fossils suggest. The domestic cats that we see today are a result of continued evolution which happened over millions of years.

Mechanics!

Cats show the most amazing feats. They have evolved in such a manner that they can twist, turn, jump and move like no other animal. In fact, the ratio of their strength to their size is much more than that of even humans. Cats do not only have great body mechanics, scientists have also observed that cats display surprising reasoning ability.

Fantastic body!

The body of the cat has developed in such a manner that it helps it to twist and turn, move and jump and do all the other tricks that you often see cats doing. The body is very soft and supple and is protected by a layer of fur. The body easily absorbs any impact. This is the reason cats don't get hurt when they fall large distances. The tail acts as a pendulum when the cats jump and helps them to maintain balance.

tail

ear   fur

whiskers

neck

Be the cat's whiskers!

These are definitely meant for cats and suit them perfectly, but they are not just decorative, as cats use their whiskers to sense obstacles or any change in the environment. Cats normally have twenty-four whiskers, twelve on each side of the nose. Whiskers are twice the thickness of the hair and are richly supplied with nerve endings, which make them very sensitive.

Clawed!

Cats use their claws for many purposes. Set in the soft ends of the fingers, claws help the cats to grip and balance themselves on many surfaces. Cats also use their claws to scratch trees and other objects and mark their territories. And most importantly, their claws help them when hunting. They are extensively used in attacking and retaining their prey.

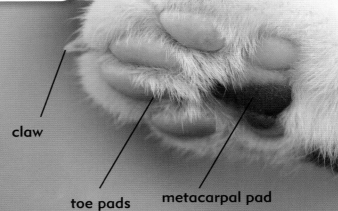

claw

toe pads   metacarpal pad

Cat Anatomy

Cats are amazing creatures with a skeletal system not very different from ours. In fact, in their small body, cats fit as many as 260 bones whereas humans manage only 206 bones. Cats have 13 ribs and humans have 12. A very interesting fact is that cats also have collar bones but unlike human collar bones, they are not attached to any other bones. Cats have very strong muscular system too, which makes them extremely strong and agile hunters.

Spiny!

You will have often seen cats in the oddest of positions – rolled as a ball, inverted 'u', straight as a line and many more shapes. What makes them so flexible? Their spine! Between each spinal vertebrae, there are discs made of fibrocartilage (fibrous tissues and cartilaginous tissues in different proportions) that are very strong but flexible. In addition, since the collar bones are attached to muscles and not bones, cats have a flexible advantage over many other animals.

Tail tale!

An anatomical wonder, the tail serves two purposes – it not only acts as a mode of communication, but it also helps the cat to maintain balance and orientation, especially when taking sharp turns, jumping and while running at a high speed. So much so for a small little tail.

Hearty!

The heart of a cat is made from hollow chambers surrounded by muscle and covered by an outer skin. The heart is divided into two halves which act as pumps. Did you know that a cat's heart beat around 120 times in a minute? At this rate, a cat's heart will beat 63 million times in a year.

Brainy!

The cat is actually a very smart animal. It has a small brain but can still demonstrate remarkable intelligence. Cats have been known to invent and use tools, play fetch, open doors and windows, they are known to use bathroom toilets as well!

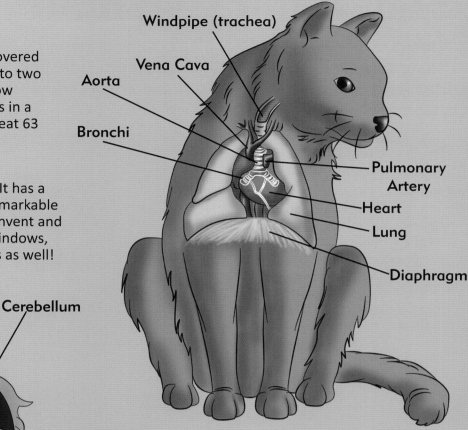

Windpipe (trachea)
Vena Cava
Aorta
Bronchi
Pulmonary Artery
Heart
Lung
Diaphragm

Cerebellum
Olfactory lobe
Optic Chiasma
Infundibulum & Hypophysis
Pons
Thalamus
Corpora Quadrigemina

Foody!

Cats have an elastic sac-like stomach which gives them a large storage capacity. The first processes digestion take place in the stomach. Then the pylorus, a muscular valve at the bottom of the stomach, pushes the remaining food into the small intestine. The digestive enzymes secreted by the small intestine break down protein and carbohydrates. Bile and pancreatic juices help to break down the food further. The body absorbs what it needs to and the rest is pushed to the large intestine. The large intestine absorbs moisture from the food and pushes the rest out of the body.

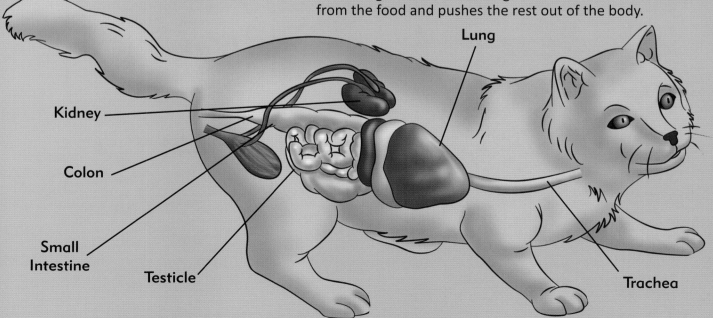

Lung
Kidney
Colon
Small Intestine
Testicle
Trachea

Sense and sensibility

For many creatures, life is all about the survival of the fittest. The same holds true for cats. Cats are equipped with senses that have been refined over years of survival and the quality of these senses set cats apart from most other animals.

Have eyes, will see!

Cats have exceptional eyesight. In fact, in the dark, they can see better than humans and they can also see ultraviolet light, which is not visible to the human eye at all. But in spite of being able to see many kinds of light, scientists believe that cats can't see colour - cats are more or less colour blind. The most important feature of the cat's eyes is the tapetum lucidum which are iridescent cells at the back of the eyeballs. These cells reflect light which make it appear that their eyes are glowing.

Have ears, will hear!

Cats can hear extremely well. And just as with their eyesight, cats are better at hearing than us. They can hear sounds at frequency levels greater than and decibel levels less than those audible to us. Cats have cupped ears which help to receive and transport sound to their ear drums. They can move their head as well as turn their ears in the direction of any sound. Cats behave very strangely when pressure is exerted on their eardrums — they swallow and stick their tongue out!

Have nose, will smell!

Cats do not rely on their olfactory senses (their sense of smell) for hunting. This is because their olfactory nerves are not as sensitive as most other animals so when it comes to smelling things, cats are very similar to humans – and they hate most of the smells that we hate! But most cats love one particular smell – that of the catnip (nepeta cataria)! It makes you wonder if it has anything to do with the word 'cat' in catnip?

Have tongue, will taste!

Cats have a long and flat tongue. Tapered at the front, the cat's tongue has papillae that help the cat to lick its body clean, and also eat even the tiniest morsel of meat on a bone or in a bowl! Cats have 470 taste buds (compared to 9000 that humans have!) which goes to explain why cats will eat almost anything. Not only do they have fewer taste buds, their buds are also not very sensitive.

Have skin and whiskers, will touch!

Whiskers and skin act as the touch sensors for cats. Cats use their whiskers (vibrissae), which are present mainly around the nose, for navigation and sensation. Whiskers are twice as thick as ordinary hair and are set three times deeper. They send signals to the nerves and to the brain which provide detailed information regarding movement, pressure and touch.

Behaviour

Cats are very intelligent creatures. They are quick learners and often remember whatever they have learnt. For example, when they find a rat hole, they look for all possible exits that the rat can use. Only when they are satisfied that there isn't any other, they sit in front of the rat hole for hours knowing the rat will come out!

Bite, grip, kill!

Cats have 30 permanent teeth. When the cat is five to seven months old, the milk teeth (a total of 26) fall out. The permanent teeth are made up of 12 incisors, four canines, 10 molars and four premolars. Cats have very sharp and fine molars and canines which help them to grip and kill their prey.

Odd, are they?

We have sometimes heard that cats get very jealous when their owners talk on the phone and make strange noises! But the fact is that they aren't jealous. They can see and hear their owner talking, but because they cannot see who they are talking to, they think their owners are talking to them and respond accordingly. Not strange at all, but cute!

Anger management!

You know a cat is irritated if it is switching its tail and if its ears are laid back. When irritation grows to anger, the cat arches its back and stiffens its body! Its hairs stand on end, and the cat starts snarling and spitting. When this anger aggravates to a fight, the cat presses its ears against its head, opens its mouth slightly with its teeth out and then jumps at its enemy.

Public display of affection!

Cats do not mind displaying affection. When a cat wants to show love, it will stiffen its body and straighten its tail and roll on the floor from one side to the other. It may also rub its head against objects and people. In cases of extreme happiness, cats may also lick people's feet and hands or may even sniff softly with its nose.

Moody?

It is very difficult to determine the various moods of cats. While on the one hand they can be extremely affectionate, gentle and soft, on the other hand, they can be very aggressive, nervous and moody! But one thing is for sure, they prefer to stay aloof and are not as friendly or social as dogs can be.

MUMMY MANIA

Have you ever thought why are there so many stray cats around? This is because cats are very fertile creatures. Cats generally produce two to three litters of kittens (one litter may have three to five kittens) in a year. Cats have a breeding span of ten years, which means that they can product up to 150 kittens in their lifetime! That is a lot of children to handle!

Brothers from different fathers!

Yes, that's right. The kittens that a cat produces in one litter can have different fathers. Female cats mate with various tomcats and can conceive while they are pregnant with another kitten. This means that in a litter of five, all the siblings could be fathered by different tomcats. Have you ever wondered why the kittens in a litter sometimes have different colours?

How many months?

Do you know how long a cat's gestation period (the time in which a baby is conceived, developed and born) is? Unlike humans, who take nine months to develop and deliver a baby, cats take anywhere between 64 to 67 days. The first litter is usually smaller than the subsequent litters.

Motherhood!

Like any other mother, cats are very protective about their young. When kittens are born, they cannot tolerate bright light, so cats deliver their babies in dark areas which receive minimal daylight. They are always ready to attack if they sense even the slightest danger around. Cats feed their kittens for round six to seven weeks (the process of gradually stopping feeding milk is called weaning). Female cats reach maturity in four to ten months whereas male cats take five to seven months.

Small world!

Kittens are very delicate when they are born. During the first ten days, kittens do very little activity. During this period they can neither see nor hear, in fact their limbs are so weak that they can barely walk. They end up crawling instead! Newborn kittens have a very small appetite. In one feed, they take in anywhere between five to twenty-five drops of milk. This would equal to one tablespoon of milk – now that's very little food!

Myth buster!

Many people believe that female white cats are not caring mothers - but this is just a myth. The reality is that female white cats with blue eyes are often deaf! So when the kittens call, they cannot hear them at all. But that doesn't stop them from being good mothers. Female white cats pick up sound vibrations and visual cues and do the most they can for their young.

TWO INTO FOUR

Cats have been around for thousands of years now but selective breeding of cats started only around hundred years ago. As cat shows became popular, people started breeding them. Soon cat breeding took the fancy of the rich and the famous, and as years passed it became a hobby for cat lovers irrespective of their background and class. Some of the cat breeds are mentioned below and it should be no surprise that now they don't look like they did hundreds of years ago.

Siamese

Siamese cats originated in Siam (now Thailand). In the 1870's, an American consul based in Bangkok sent a Siamese cat to the then American President as a gift. That was the Siamese cat's first foreign visit. After that, they never looked back! They come to the UK in the 1880's and to many other parts of the world thereafter. Siamese cats are of two types: traditional Siamese and modern Siamese. Siamese cats are temperamental, playful, active and very intelligent.

Persian

The oldest-known pedigree cat breed award goes to none other than the Persian cat! Many people think of a Persian cat as being only white but Persian cats come in many different colours. Did you know they have at least 60 colour variations? Persian cats are very popular as pets because they are very gentle. They are not only playful and affectionate, but they are easy to look after which makes them very desirable.

Abyssinian

One of the top five most popular cat breeds in the world, the Abyssinian cat (also known as Aby) has its origin in Egypt. It was only brought to the UK in the 19th century after which it became popular all over the world. They are very curious cats so it is advisable to close and lock cupboards if you own one of these cats. Abys also have a very 'cry-baby' attitude – they are attention seekers and will do anything until they get it!

Burmese

Strangely, Burmese cats do not originate from Burma but from Thailand! So Siamese and Burmese cats share the same origin. It was only when they arrived in Burma that they got their name. Burmese cats are extremely affectionate, caring, lovable and gentle. They love to be around their owner and are known to do various stunts in order to entertain them. Next time you want to recommend a cat to a friend, you know which one to advise!

Himalayan

Where did the Himalayan cats come from? Definitely not the Himalayas! The first Himalayan cats were born to Persian and Siamese parents. In fact, had it not been for their blue eyes and colouration, you could have mistaken them for Persian cats. Well, all of us resemble our parents and ancestors.

Main Coon

Recognised officially by the International Cat Association, the Main Coon is the second most popular cat breed of the world. No one knows for sure when and where the first Main Coon was born! Although they look ferocious, Main Coons are the most social and friendly of cats. They love people and like being in their company. Main Coon is, in reality, a very sociable animal!

FUR TYPES

Did you think only humans have many different hair styles? Not so! Cats have different hair types (fur types) too and are also known for the kind of fur they have. Numerous variations can be found in the fur types of domestic cats – some due to natural evolution and some due to selective breeding. Three types of hairs in the fur – down, awn and guard – make each cat look different from other breeds. Did you know that cats moult throughout the year and their winter coats are longer than their summer coats?

Down Awn & Guard?

The innermost layer of the fur is made of down hairs. They are the shortest hairs of the body. Awn hairs are the next level of hairs that protect the down hairs. They are thinner than the guard hairs, which are the primary hairs of a cat's coat. Guard hairs are the longest hairs of the coat and make up the top most layer.

Long-haired Cats!

Long-haired cats have been around since the 1500's. The length of the hairs depends on the breed and also the season with the length of the hairs in winter longer than in summer. A cat's guard hairs give its coat length, whereas the down hair insulates the cat's body. For example, the Persian longhair has very long guard hairs and very thick down hairs which make its coat appear very thick.

Short-haired Cats!

As the name suggests, short-haired cats do not have very long hairs in their coat. They generally have very soft, fine coats which act as a thin cover. The Manx, for example, has very short and thick down hairs which are covered by guard hairs which are not very long either. Similarly, the British short has a short fine coat that stands out from the body.

Bald or almost bald?

Not all cats have either a long or short coat of hairs. Have you ever seen a Sphynx, not the pyramid, but the cat! It appears to be hairless, but in reality, it is not. It has a very fine layer of very small hairs which are hardly visible, and it also has whiskers and eyebrows. The lack of thick cover means that the Sphynx has no protection against extreme heat or cold. To keep itself warm, the Sphynx is often seen cuddling with other animals or people.

Semi-long-haired Cats!

There are long-haired cats, there are short-haired cats, there are no-hair cats and there are also semi-long-haired cats! The semi-long-haired cats have very long guard hairs and very fine down hairs. This means that their coats do not appear as thick as that of the long-haired cats. Semi-long-haired cats, such as the Maine Coon, display different hair lengths in different seasons.

FUR COLOUR

How many different coloured cats do you recall seeing? Lots! Domestic cats come in many colours and patterns. Tabby, or striped coat, is the most common colouration pattern found in cats. The presence or absence of melanin – the pigment that decides the colour of hair or skin – is primarily responsible for the colour of the cat's coat but it also depends on light conditions. Excess light lightens the colour of the coat or makes it appear lighter than usual.

Selfish!

Self coloured cats have coats that have a colour which is solid from the root to the tip. There is no dilution or fading. There are four basic colours of self-coloured cats – black, chocolate, cinnamon and red. All other self colours are modifications of these colours but follow the same basic principle – the colour is solid from root to tip. You may be wondering why white has not been mentioned as a self colour. That is because white is not a colour but the absence of it.

Diluted!

As the name suggests, some colours have been diluted to make new colours. The difference between modified self colours and diluted colours is that unlike modified self colours, diluted colours are not solid from root to tip. Some areas have less pigment than other areas which make them look paler. Therefore, a light and dark pattern appears on the coat. For example, cream is a dilute of red. But not all creams appear the same; some creams are redder than others.

Tipped!

In tipped cats, the tip of guard hairs and the awn hairs are a shade which is different to the main colour. The down hairs could be of single colour but the tipping of guard and awn hairs gives the cat a different look altogether. If you look at the British shorthair tipped cats, which first appeared tipped in the 1970's, you will see that most of them are white or silver with black tips, though many other colours of tips are popular now.

Shaded!

Shading is an extended form of tipping. In tipping, only the tip of the hair is a different colour, but in shading, the colouring extends much farther down the length of the hair. The down hairs are generally white, but almost half the length of the awn and guards hairs have a different colour. When the cat walks or moves, the white of the down hairs is visible giving the coat a very different look.
For example, the Shaded Silver Persian has a white undercoat as compared to the pure white undercoat of the Persian cats. Their overcoat has black shading which gives them a salt-and-pepper look.

Smoked!

This is the most extreme form of tipping where a large part of the overcoat is pigmented. One can say that the original colour is tipped at the root and the new colour makes up the main colour of the hairs. The down hairs are lighter than the 'smoking' and as in the case of shaded cats, the difference is most visible when the cat is moving or walking.

Ticked!

Ticking is the most helpful to cats as a means of camouflage. In ticked cats, colours appear in bands. The original colour followed by the added pigment followed by the original colour and so on. In some tabby cats, the colour is solid, and the banding in some hairs is not visible. This is called disruptive colouration.

COAT PATTERN

Most coat patterns reflect the tabby markings of their ancestors in some way. There could be variations but the basic patterns remain the same. Breeders devote a lot of time to select a coat pattern and there are two plus points of breeding in this case – breeders can do away with unwanted characteristics and add special qualities by following a well-designed patterning programme. It takes a lot of time and luck to develop a cat with an ideal coat patterning. Coat patterns do not generally change much after birth (there are few exceptions) but it may become more distinctive.

Particolours!

Many cats have coats that have significant areas of white fur along with other colours. The Calico, with clearly defined areas of black, white, red and cream, and the bicoloured, with white and another colour, are examples of particoloured cats. By specialised breeding, the white area in particoloured cats' bodies has been restricted to half of the body so that both colours are equally visible.

Tortoiseshell!

This does not mean that the cats have coats made of tortoise shells! Tortoiseshell cats, or 'torties', have red; brown or black, and chocolate, cream or cinnamon evenly distributed over their bodies. One variation of the tortoiseshell cats is the blue cream variety where cream and blue, lilac or fawn colours are added for a different colour. For some genetic reason, almost all tortoiseshell cats are female!

Pointed!

Pointed cats stand out because of their special markings. The extremities of their bodies – face, ears, legs, feet and tail – have a colour which is much darker than the base colour. For example, the Siamese pointed cats are conspicuously coloured – they have a white body with black ends! The colours of the points can depend upon the body temperature of the cat, the climate it is found in and the length of it fur. One variation of pointed cats is the Van pattern where only the tail and a part of the cat's head is coloured.

Tabby!

Tabby is the most common of coat patterns found in cats. Most stray cats have tabby pattern on their coats, and not only domestic cats but many wild cats have the tabby pattern too! Tabby cats have an advantage over others when it comes to camouflage. There are many variations in the tabby pattern, such as the classic tabby, the spotted tabby, and so on. Also known as blotched tabbies, the classic tabbies have black, brown and ochre lines on their bodies with patterns like a butterfly on the shoulder. Rings on the tail are also very common to classic tabbies. Spotted tabbies do not have distinct lines but oval, round or rosette-shaped spots on their bodies.

HOME SWEET HOME!

Cats can live anywhere and everywhere! They are also found on islands which are currently uninhabited where they survive because they are extremely independent and self-reliant creatures. The only place where cats are not found is Antarctica – they will probably need a thicker fur coat before they can live there.

Available everywhere!

Be it forests, grassland, desert, tundra, scrubland, wetland or coastal areas, cats can be found everywhere. They adapt themselves to any environment they are in.

Agricultural lands!

They are found here too - but not to grow crops. Most of these cats are owned by farmers and encouraged onto the fields so that they can protect their crops from rats and other pests. To feed one cat is simpler that feeding a horde of rats!

Cities!

Cats are very common in cities, and not just as pets. Many stray cats can be seen roaming around and they fend for themselves as easily as any other animals. You will always find them around bins and other areas where they can find food and scraps for themselves.

And then your home...

That's the best place a cat can be – a place in your home and most importantly, a place in your heart! And once there, it will just settle in more and more.

Bedding!

Give your cat a bed – if you don't have a cat bed, a cushion and a sheet would do, but don't expect it to sleep there. More often than not, you will find your cat in your bed!

Littering!

Don't forget the litter tray - a nice and clean tray, that is. If you don't know it already, cats hate dirty litter trays. In fact, if you find your puss in a fowl mood, check its litter tray. It might be dirty!

Bowling!

And don't forget to keep a bowl of clean water for you cat. It will lap some whenever it feels thirsty.

CAT FOOD

Dogs have been provided with specialised food for a long time, but specialised food for cats wasn't available until much later. One possible reason for it could be the fact that cats are very self dependent and can hunt and scavenge!

Nice mice!

Cats love mice - all of us know that. How happy it feels depends upon how often a cat can catch its favourite food too.

Snakes?!

Yes, some cats are known to eat small snakes too! Now, how snaky is that!

Insects!

Many cats eat certain insects such as cicadas. They can eat their favourite insect as often as they catch them - which can be quite tricky!

Milky white!

Cats love to drink milk from time to time. Give them a bowl and you will see how quickly they lick it clean, but be aware that many cats will get an upset stomach by drinking milk.

Fishies!

Cats love fish too! Notice where your cat loiters when your mum makes that special fish meal for you. It will be hovering around the kitchen to taste whatever it can lay its paws on!

Dry food!

There are many types of food that cat food specialists make. Some of them are dry foods which has all the nutrition – carbohydrates, fats, proteins and vitamins – that cats require and are flavoured to make the food more tempting for them!

Wet Food!

Wet food, or canned food, especially fish, is readily available for cats.

Apart from these foods, cats will eat anything they like! There is no hard and fast rule to their eating pattern, but most of them dislike oranges and lemons!

I WANT A CAT!

Once you have decided you want a cat, half the work is done, but the difficult half remains. How to choose a cat? There are various questions that need answering - what breed, what colour, coat length, pattern and body type? And the biggest question of all - how much maintenance will your cat need? Your cat store owner or breeder will help you with all of these questions but try to make a list of questions before you meet them. You don't want to miss out anything.

Pedigree or non-pedigree?

Whether you want a pedigree or a non-pedigree cat is entirely up to you. Keep in mind that non-pedigree cats are easier to find and cheaper. If you want a pedigree cat, check your local newspaper for breeders offering kittens for sale or call one of the cat associations or specialist breed societies.

How long will my cat live?

Both pedigree and non-pedigree cats can live up to 15 years. It depends on the diet and medical care and attention you give to your cat as and when they need it.

Temperament?

This is another important thing you should keep in mind when choosing a cat. For example, don't get a shy, reserved cat if you have kids or other pets in your household. Similarly don't get an energetic, people-oriented, loving cat if you are going to be away from the house for long periods.

Long-haired or short-haired?

Another important choice, but remember that long-haired cats require more grooming than short-haired ones. So if you don't have time to spend on your cat, go for a short-haired one. And if you can give some time to your cat religiously every day, go for a long haired one.

Colour?

Entirely up to you. But remember that as beautiful as they may look, whites need much more maintenance than other colours.

Male or female?

Your choice again, but keep in mind that in many breeds, the males are slightly larger than the females. Whatever you buy, remember to neuter the male or spay the female. It helps their temperament; and also, you do not want unwanted kittens running around.

Out to buy...

When you have decided on all the above, call a breeder and arrange a visit. Whilst there, observe the kitten for some time to gauge its behaviour. Then check its coat, tail, paws, ears, eyes and mouth. If you are satisfied with your kitten, you may want to call for a vet and let him examine it, just to be sure, especially if you are paying a lot of money.

GETTING THE CAT READY

There are certain times in a year when many cat owners want to enter their cats into a competition. But there is a lot of preparation that goes into getting a cat ready for a show.

LONG-HAIRED

Combing!

You should groom your cat regularly, whether you want to show your cat or not. Combing the hairs of cats on a regular basis is very important to keep their fur in top condition. Combing also helps to get rid of ticks, lice and fleas.

Cleaning!

Start with a brush to take out dead hairs. Then take a swab of cotton to clean the eyes, ears and nose of your cat. Then use a smaller brush like a toothbrush to brush the hairs of the face. Brush out the hairs of the neck till it forms a ruff. Nails need to be cleaned and trimmed - this should be done by a professional.

Powdering!

Sprinkle some non-toxic grooming powder to keep the coat dry. Make sure that the powder is evenly spread over the body. When it's time to take the excess powder off, use a bristle brush and brush out the coat until there are no traces of powder left.

SHORT-HAIRED

Bran-ning!

The best way to clean short-haired cats is by giving them a bran wash. Rub them in bran to remove extra grease and dirt, and then brush the bran out. If your cat doesn't like bran, use a good shampoo. Don't forget to apply a good conditioner after that. After the cleaning process is over, use a towel and pat it dry.

Cleaning!

Use a cotton swab and a mild salt solution to clean the area near the eyes, nose and ears. Remember to not poke them in the eye! Use vet nail clippers to carefully trim the nails.

Brushing!

Use a rubber brush to brush the soft hairs of your cat. But don't brush it too hard otherwise it might harm the undercoat.

For both long-haired and short-haired cats, you can polish their coat with a polishing mitt that has chamois leather on one side and velvet on the other. If you do not have a polishing mitt, use a piece of silk. The shining effect is almost the same.

HAVE IT, WILL FLAUNT IT!

If you are of the opinion that only pedigree cats can be taken to cat shows, you are mistaken. Even non-pedigree cats can be shown, and with great popularity!

When's the show?

If you want to show your cat, the first thing you need to do is to find out when the next show is scheduled. Cat shows are advertised in enthusiast magazines.

Before applying!

You apply for a form, fill it in and submit it to the organisation. But before you apply, make sure you are ready for the show. Keep in mind:

1. Read all the rules and regulations of the show and apply only if you accept the terms of the show.
2. Make sure your cat is vaccinated before the show. If it is not, it will be disqualified. And in any case, you don't want to spread or catch any germs!
3. Remember that pregnant and lactating cats cannot be shown.

Travel!

Make sure your cat is into the habit of travelling before you travel to the venue of the show. Your cat should not be sick by the end of the journey as this will spoil all your plans.

Contact!

Get in touch with the organisation conducting the show. If you have any queries, they will be happy to help. Decide whether you want to show your cat in that particular show or not.

Prepare!

After you have applied, get your cat ready for the show. Regular grooming is very important so that your cat looks its best. Get the cage, the furnishings, collars etc. ready.

Prepare your cat to be handled by others. It is very important and will earn points for your cat.

At the venue!

When you get to the venue, your cat will be given a numbered badge. Wait for your cat's turn and while you are waiting, check its ears, eyes, nose and tail for dirt.

Judge calling!

When your cat's number is called out, take it to the stage and place it in the cage with a corresponding number. Put a litter tray and a bowl of water in the cage so that your cat is comfortable.

And the winner is...

If your cat wins, it will be awarded a rosette. Purebreds can compete for the champion titles whereas household cats compete for Master and Grand Master titles.

Cats in Detail

Black Silver Abyssinian

Introduction: Also known as Abys or Bunny cats, Abyssinians are considered to be the cats the ancient Egyptians worshipped because they resemble the mummified cats discovered by archaeologists. Abyssinians come in many varieties, Black Silver Abyssinian being one of them.

Appearance: The down hairs and the under-parts of Black Silver Abyssinians are white. The hind legs, tip of the tail and the spine are solid black. No third colour, especially yellow, is desired in Silver Black Abyssinians.

Behaviour: Like most Abyssinians, Silver Black Abyssinians are very intelligent, adaptable and friendly. They are generally very fond of their owner, but need open space to live.

Factastic:
Black Silver Abyssinians have caught the eye of cat fanciers and are being developed to very high standards in New Zealand and Britain.

Ancestry	Introduced in	Coat length	Coat Colour	Fur Type
Non-pedigree Ticked Shorthairs	Great Britain in 1860's	Short	Silver and black. Yellow is not preferred	Soft, silky and ticked

Ruddy Abyssinian

Introduction: Ruddys, like all other Abys, are special tabby cats. Their beautiful ticked coats and their characteristic M-shaped frown mark on the forehead make them a class apart from normal tabbies.

Appearance: Ruddy Aby is also known as Tawny or Usual Aby. It has the most popular colour. The rich golden brown with brighter orange towards the root is what makes the Ruddy so special. It has red nose, black or brown paw pads and large ears that are ticked with brown or black.

Behaviour: Like all Abys, Ruddys are very active and alert. You cannot move an inch in their territory without them noticing you.

Factastic:
There is also a wild variety of the Ruddy Abyssinian. Unlike domestic Abyssinians, they were discovered as recently as 1980's and their country of origin is Singapore!

Ancestry	Introduced in	Coat length	Coat Colour	Fur Type
Non-pedigree Ticked Shorthairs	Great Britain in 1860's	Short	Rich golden brown ticked with various shades of darker brown or black	Soft, silky and ticked

Sorrel Abyssinian

Introduction: Sorrel Abyssinians are often also called Red Abyssinians but they are not really red but more of an apricot colour. Breeders are making attempts to develop a variety which is a more genuine red.

Appearance: Endowed with amber eyes and a long elegant neck, Sorrel Abyssinians are one of the most elegant-looking cats. Sorrels have an apricot base colour with a darker top coat.

Behaviour: Like all Abyssinian cats, Sorrel Abys are very playful. They are very mischievous when they are young but tend to mellow as they grow older and go on to live until about twelve years old.

Factastic:
Like most Abys, Sorrel Abys do not like to sit on the lap. They would rather perch on their owner's shoulders. And they love water!

Ancestry	Introduced in	Coat length	Coat Colour	Fur Type
Non-pedigree Ticked Shorthairs	Great Britain in 1860's	Short	'Sorrel' red	Soft, silky and ticked

American Bobtail

Introduction: A short-tailed brown tabby male and a Siamese coloured cat produced the first ever American Bobtail. The American Bobtail is one of the more recent breeds to have been accepted for the championships by the Cat Fanciers' Association.

Appearance: The bobtail is called so because its tail is 'bobbed' to almost half of a normal cat's tail's length. The American Bobtail's tail length varies between two to four inches. The cat looks so muscular and athletic that people often mistake it to be a wild cat.

Behaviour: Intelligent, friendly, alert and playful, American bobtails are much like dogs and are often seen playing fetch with their owners! Very easy to train, they are known to be extremely fond of their owners.

Factastic:
American Bobtails are knows to relieve stress and psychotherapists have been known to use them in their treatments due to their good behaviour and extreme sensitivity to humans under stress.

Ancestry	Introduced in	Coat length	Coat Colour	Fur Type
Short-tailed brown tabby and seal-point Siamese	USA in 1970's	Short	Fawn and white, blue tabby, red tabby and white	Soft undercoat and a hard overcoat

Black American Curl

Introduction: American Curls are known for their ears which 'curl' backwards. When kittens are born, their ears are not curled, but within a week, their ears curl tightly and remain so for around five months. After that the curl opens up. The extent of the final curl varies from cat to cat. Some cats do not develop curls at all.

Appearance: Black American Curls have a very fine silky coat with almost no undercoat and no ruff. They have a beautiful plumed tail which is very wide at the base and tapers at the tip. They have thick legs with rounded paws.

Behaviour: Black American Curls, like all the other American Curls, are very friendly and playful. They are known to behave as kittens even in their adulthood. These cats are very affectionate and are always ready to make friends.

Factastic:

A pet quality American Curl may have almost straight ears, but cats bred for showing must have ears that curl anywhere between 90 and 180 degrees. A greater angle is preferable in shows, but there is a catch – a cat whose ears touch the back of its skull is disqualified! So watch the curl!

Ancestry	Introduced in	Coat length	Coat Colour	Fur Type
	United States of America in 1981	Short	Black	Silky

Black and White American Curl

Introduction: All American Curls trace their origin to Shulamith, the first know Long hair American curl that was discovered by Grace and Joe Ruga outside their parking lot. The owners bred many varieties of long hair American Curls and later bred short hair options too using a domestic cat in their breeding programme.

Appearance: Black and White American Curls have a semi-long overcoat with a fine and soft undercoat. Because the coat is not thick, the cat does not require a lot of maintenance. Even while changing coats, it does not shed a lot of hairs.

Behaviour: They are said to be not 'catty' at all. A cat that doesn't like to quarrel is definitely not catty. These cats like to make friends with other cats and are often seen training their kittens.

Factastic:

Grace and Joe Ruga found Shulamith in 1981 in Southern California. What surprised them was the fact that Shulamith's first litter had two curly eared kittens!

Ancestry	Introduced in	Coat length	Coat Colour	Fur Type
Non-pedigree Curl	United States of America in 1981	Short	Black and white	Silky and soft

Brown Mackerel Tabby and White American Curl

Introduction: Many breeds of domestic cat are used in the breeding program of American Curls. As a result of this, the new breeds take many good genes from their parents and hence, are healthy and strong.

Appearance: Mackerel tabbies have lines that run parallel down the sides of the coat. All American Curls are medium sized cats with slender, elongated bodies. The medium sized head has a wedge shaped pattern on it.

Behaviour: Curls are quiet cats. They do not like to make noise unnecessarily but when communicating, they make thrilling noises. They love to play and they will find any object tempting to play with – watch out for all your toys!

Factastic:
The 'belief' that the curls were a result of a disease or a deformity is merely a myth. These curls are a much desired characteristic and a cat fancier will tell you the worth of those curls.

Ancestry	Introduced in	Coat length	Coat Colour	Fur Type
Non-pedigree Curl	United States of America in 1981	Semi-long	Brown and White	Silky

Seal Lynx Point American Curl

Introduction: An ideal American Curl would be medium sized, alert, intelligent with a sweet expression. Everything else would be taken care of by having wonderful ears.

Appearance: The Seal Lynx Point has dark brown patches and a body colour that could range anywhere between ivory and light brown (seal point). The brown patches appear in a tabby pattern on the legs (lynx point). These cats have tipped tails and blue eyes.

Behaviour: American Curls take a long time to mature – almost up to three years as opposed to other cats who mature much faster.

Factastic:
People always confuse the American Curl with the American Fold. But there is a big difference between the two – American Curl's ears curl backwards whereas the American Fold's ears fold forwards!

Ancestry	Introduced in	Coat length	Coat Colour	Fur Type
Non-pedigree Curl	USA in 1981	Short	Ivory to light brown	Silky and fine with little undercoat

Silver Classic Tabby American shorthair

Introduction: American shorthairs are descendants of the Europeans cats that were brought to North America by European settlers.
They carried these cats on board their ships to get rid of rats!

Appearance: The Silver Classic Tabby has typical black tabby marks on a silvery-white background. The tabby rings on the tail are dark and those around the neck look like the cat is wearing a necklace! The pattern on the body is symmetrical on both sides of the body.

Behaviour: The American Shorthairs have not forgotten their origins. Their ancestors were used for hunting rats and this trait is predominant in their behaviour today.

Factastic:
Earlier known as Domestic Shorthairs, American Shorthairs got their new name after the Silver Tabby won the US Cat of the Year award in 1965!

Ancestry	Introduced in	Coat length	Coat Colour	Fur Type
Non-pedigree Shorthairs	United States of America in 1600's	Short	Silver and black	Thick and hard

White Angora

Introduction: The Angoras originated in Turkey and were named after the capital city of Angora (Ankara). But the original Angoras vanished many years ago. The Angoras that we now know are the ones which have been bred by using the Oriental Shorthair for the longhair gene.

Appearance: There are two kinds of White Angoras – green eyed and blue eyed. White Angoras have large pointed ears, long slender neck, and a very slender but strong body. Their wedge-shaped head adds to their elegance.

Behaviour: White Angoras are playful and friendly and take every opportunity to show their affection to their owners. Turkish Angoras are very intelligent, so much so that the owners do not need to train them; they can train their owners!

Factastic:
Odd-eyed White Angora cats(with one blue eye and one green or yellow or brown) can be deaf on the side of the blue eye! But not every odd-eyed White Angora has this problem.

Ancestry	Introduced in	Coat length	Coat Colour	Fur Type
White Oriental Shorthair	Great Britain in 1960's	Longhair	White	Fine and silky

Bengal Leopard

Introduction: What happens when a breeding programme involves a domestic cat and a wild cat? The beautiful coat of a domestic breed with the markings of a wild cat, is produced. Bengal Leopards, the offspring of a male domestic cat and a female Asian Leopard cat, is one such breed.

Appearance: The Bengal Leopard is known for its rosette-spotted coat which is very different from the coat of a regular spotted tabby. The rosettes are spread horizontally on the body and achieve their true colour at around a year old. Bengal Leopards have very sensitive ears and can pick up the smallest of the sound, thanks to their 'wild' genes.

Behaviour: Bengal Leopards are known for their intelligence and playfulness. They not only love their owner who they love to follow around, they also love any other pet in the house and are often seen cuddling with them.

Factastic:
Bengal Leopards are particularly fond of water. Their love for water is so great that they have been known to jump into the shower with their owners!

Ancestry	Introduced in	Coat length	Coat Colour	Fur Type
Asian Leopard Cat Crosses	United States of America in 1963	Semi-long	Sorrel or Mink tabby	Dense, silky and soft

Chocolate point Birman

Introduction: Birmans are often confused with the Burmese cat – but be aware, they are two different species. Birmans, often called the 'Sacred Cat of Burma'. Birmans have semi-long hair, light coloured bodies with darker coloured points. The people of Burma believe that their origin is legendary.

Appearance: As the name suggests, Chocolate point Birmans have 'points' – tail, face, ears, parts of legs – in a chocolate colour. In some cases, a bit of chocolate shading can been seen on the body as well. The nose of Chocolate point Birmans is brown and they generally have deep-blue eyes.

Behaviour: Birmans are very curious by nature and help to prove Murphy 's Law – if something can go wrong, it will go wrong. Birmans are known to get involved in any and every kind of 'action' and inadvertently find themselves in trouble.

Factastic:

Burmese legend has it that the earliest Birmans were found around the sacred temple of the Goddess Tsun-Kyan-Kse – represented by a golden statue and blue sapphire eyes – centuries ago. It was believed that the white cats were the souls of dead priests who were guarding the temple.

Ancestry	Introduced in	Coat length	Coat Colour	Fur Type
Non-pedigree cats	Burma (Myanmar)	Semi-long	Ivory with chocolate points	Silky

Cream point Birman

Introduction: The first Birmans were Seal point Birmans but many more forms were developed later. Cream point Birman is one such form. Birmans are medium-sized, muscular cats and are known for their stunning expressions.

Appearance: The contrast in colour is not apparent in Cream point Birmans for obvious reasons – cream points on an ivory body are not very distinct, but it is hard to miss the ivory 'gloves' on the legs. The golden hue on the points makes this form look very elegant.

Behaviour: On the one hand, Birmans are very curious but on the other hand, they are very reserved and prefer to keep quiet until they are hungry. A character of contrasts or a balanced behaviour?

Factastic:

There is another myth surrounding the Birmans. Once a priest of the temple was attacked by robbers. In his bid to save the temple, the priest died and his soul entered Sinh, his faithful companion. The cat transformed instantly – the eyes turned blue and the coat turned to white with golden hues as of the goddess with brown points - the colour of the earth. This probably was the origin of the Seal Point Birmans.

Ancestry	Introduced in	Coat length	Coat Colour	Fur Type
Non-pedigree Curl	Burma (Myanmar)	Semi-long	Ivory with cream points and golden hue	Silky

Red point Birman

Introduction: Birmans are usually very healthy and live up to fifteen years of age. They do not even need a lot of maintenance – single-layer coat means the fur doesn't get tangled and combing isn't a necessity (though grooming on a regular basis is good for all cats); and they can be bathed once every six weeks. That is very low maintenance, indeed.

Appearance: The Red point Birman is a recent addition the Birman group. Red point Birmans display an identical pattern of markings. Orange points on the front paws are covered by symmetrical, straight white lines. The hind paws are covered in white in full.

Behaviour: If you are looking for a pet, a Birman will be your best companion. Serene, quiet, affectionate and playful, Birmans are a pleasure to be with. They are known to get along with children and other pets as well.

Ancestry	Introduced in	Coat length	Coat Colour	Fur Type
Non-pedigree Curl	Burma (Myanmar)	Semi-long	Ivory with red points	Silky

Factastic:
The first trip any Birman made abroad was in 1919. Two Birmans – a male and a female – were taken to France. The male died en route, but the female, Sita, who was pregnant, survived. She gave birth to Poupee, a perfect Birman female.

Seal Tortie Point Birman

Introduction: Developing Birmans is a difficult task in itself considering the kind of precision pointing required, but developing a tortie is all the more difficult. Consider adding other equally distributed colours to the pointing!

Appearance: The body colour of a Seal Tortie Point Birman is fawn and it has brown or red points. Since it is a tortie, it has shades ranging from soft brown to red spread evenly on the back and side of its body.

Behaviour: Birmans are very smart. Not even the butter is safe in the butter-dish. Your Birman knows where exactly it is! Try locking your cupboards – that might help to keep things safe!

Factastic:
When a seal point is mated with a tortie point, a male red point or a female seal tortie point is born.

Ancestry	Introduced in	Coat length	Coat Colour	Fur Type
Non-pedigree cats	Burma (Myanmar)	Semi-long	Fawn with red or brown shades and points	Silky

Blue Lynx Point Birman

Introduction: Since Birmans lose their fur in the summer months, their appearance changes from season to season. Don't expect a silky haired Birman right after a long hot summer!

Appearance: Lynx markings are tabby markings where agouti, the light and dark alternating pattern along the length of each hair of the coat, is unmasked. Many cats can have lynx markings, but you can get a lynx point only if at least one of the parents is a lynx cat.

Behaviour: Birman are very gentle cats. They live as comfortably in an apartment as in a bungalow; and though they love the outdoors, they shouldn't be let out alone considering their gentle nature – not all animals roaming outdoors are as gentle as a Birman.

Factastic:
Poupee, the kitten born to Sita, was handed over to Monsieur Baudoin de Crevoisier, the first Birman breeder. The first kitten Sita produced was fathered by a Siamese male.

Ancestry	Introduced in	Coat length	Coat Colour	Fur Type
Non-pedigree cats	Burma (Myanmar)	Semi-long	Bluish white with blue points	Silky

Seal Lynx Point Birman

Introduction: All Birmans are born with a whitish coat. The cat gets its point colour anywhere between two days to two weeks after birth, but the full colour shows only with time, and a full growth of hair takes almost three years!

Appearance: So many Birmans! How do you know which one is your Seal Lynx Point Birman? Look for the one which has lynx markings above the white on the hind legs. The tabby 'M' marking on the forehead is also very clear in this cat. The beige body has golden hues and seal brown points.

Behaviour: Birmans are known for their intelligence and are believed to have good memory. Once they have seen you keeping their favourite toy somewhere, they will remember that hiding place for life. And every time you think the toy is well hidden, you will be sadly mistaken!

Factastic:
Birmans have 'spectacled' or 'kohl-lined' eyes! See it for yourself!

Ancestry	Introduced in	Coat length	Coat Colour	Fur Type
Non-pedigree cats	Burma (Myanmar)	Semi-long	Beige with seal brown points	Silky

Seal Tortie Lynx Point Birman

Introduction: Creation of a seal lynx point means that the cat will have both red and lynx gene colours as well as a lynx pattern. This makes it possible to have a Seal Tortie Lynx Point. Introduction of these two genes increases the colour choice in Birmans from four to twenty.

Appearance: The addition of tortie to tabby is very visible in Seal Tortie Lynx Point Birmans. Both tabby and tortie are visible alongside, although the markings are not very significant. The fawn body has an even distribution of light brown or red on the back and flanks.

Behaviour: Birmans are curious and playful, but if you are busy and your Birman knows it, it will not disturb you at all. It will sit at your feet without making a sound. After all, it wants your company first – talking is not essential.

Factastic:
Did you know Seal Tortie Point Birmans do not have any brothers – they are an all girls group! Yes, they are a female-only breed. Remember we discussed earlier that all torties are female!

Ancestry	Introduced in	Coat length	Coat Colour	Fur Type
Non-pedigree cats	Burma (Myanmar)	Semi-long	Fawn with seal brown points	Silky

Blue-eyed White British shorthair

Introduction: If you were to draw a big circle, a British shorthair's face would fit in it exactly – that is how rounded their face is. They are also known for their bulky size. The three forms of the British Shorthair, distinguished by colour are – Golden-eyed, Blue-Eyed and Odd-Eyed.

Appearance: The first Blue-eyed British Shorthair was seen somewhere around the 1900's in a cat show. It was a featured winner in many shows around that time. The cat has large, rounded, deep-blue eyes, which are its most distinct characteristic.

Behaviour: These cats are considered gentle giants for their size and nature. They are very affectionate and quiet. You will never see a White British shorthair get into trouble because they are the least inquisitive of all cats!

Factastic:
Blue-eyed White British shorthairs are generally deaf but some are found to have good aural senses.

Ancestry	Introduced in	Coat length	Coat Colour	Fur Type
Non-pedigree shorthairs	Great Britain in 1880's	Short	White	Short, dense and firm

Golden-eyed White British shorthair

Introduction: Though many new colours, such as lilac, are now being developed, these cats are preferred in their original colour, especially white. But being pure white in colour with not even a hint of yellow or any other tinge, exposes these cats to the dangers of getting sunburn.

Appearance: As the name suggests, this bulky cat with deep chest and broad shoulders generally has golden-coloured eyes. But the colour can vary from a deep gold to an orange or copper.

Behaviour: The good thing about them is although they are friendly, they do like to be on their own. They do no crave attention and will be happy to leave you alone to do your own thing.

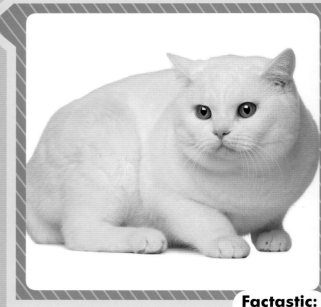

Factastic:
White cats have always been more popular than their black counterparts. Why? Because in many societies, black cats are considered evil.

Ancestry	Introduced in	Coat length	Coat Colour	Fur Type
Non-pedigree shorthairs	Great Britain in 1880's	Short	White	Short, dense and firm

British longhair

Introduction: The British longhair was created to be a different longhair option for the British shorthair, where the only option for years had been the Persian cat. But when the Exotic Shorthair was developed as a counterpart for the Persian, breeders decided to create one especially for the British shorthair.

Appearance: British longhairs have all the same physical characteristic as the British shorthair, except the length of the fur. In spite of so much effort put into breeding the longhair, it has still not been officially recognised in the UK.

Behaviour: British longhairs are gentle and nice, and like shorthairs, they like to be alone. You will not be disturbed. They do enjoy the company of other longhairs, if they find any!

Factastic:
The British longhair is known as the Lowlander in the Netherlands and the Britannia in Europe.

Ancestry	Introduced in	Coat length	Coat Colour	Fur Type
Non-pedigree shorthairs	Great Britain in 1870's	Long	Various	Dense and firm

Black British shorthair

Introduction: Black British Shorthairs have been common in cat shows since the early 1900's. They lost their popularity for a brief period during the World Wars but came back in full in the 1950's.

Appearance: Short and stout, Black British Shorthairs are stunning to look at. What adds to their striking looks are their eyes – copper, orange or deep gold in colour.

Behaviour: Black British Shorthairs are very easy going cats. They do not mind staying indoors which makes them very suitable for people who live in apartments or small houses.

Factastic:
Remember not to sunbathe your Black British Shorthair much. A lot of sun might bleach the colour and change it to a rusty brown!

Ancestry	Introduced in	Coat length	Coat Colour	Fur Type
Non-pedigree shorthairs	Great Britain in 1880's	Short	Black	Short, dense and firm

Blue British shorthair

Introduction: The most popular of all colours is the blue coloured British Shorthair. During the wars, this cat had almost become extinct but since then their numbers have begun to rise.

Appearance: The Blue British Shorthair is fatter than the other fat shorthairs! Breeders put in a lot of effort to maintain an even shade in the coat so that no tabby markings are visible..

Behaviour: British shorthairs are very playful. They typically like to play with mouse or stick-style toys.

Factastic:
For a very long time, the Persians were the most popular cats in Britain, but things changed in 2001 when the British Shorthair became the most popular cat registered by the UK's Governing Council of Cat Registry.

Ancestry	Introduced in	Coat length	Coat Colour	Fur Type
Non-pedigree shorthairs	Great Britain in 1880's	Short	Blue	Short, dense and firm

Chocolate British shorthair

Introduction: British Shorthairs are said to have a 'cracking' coat. This is because the coat breaks very finely over the contours of the body. Male British Shorthairs are bigger than the females.

Appearance: Chocolate is not a very commonly found colour in British Shorthairs. Though tabby marking can be found in some kittens, none can be found in adult cats.

Behaviour: British Shorthairs are not destructive at all – rest assured that your house is in safe 'paws' when you are out at work. Your cat will busy itself and will not generally ruin things around the house.

Factastic:
The Chocolate Persian was used to breed the Chocolate British Shorthair. It is still a young colour and is not recognised by many associations.

Ancestry	Introduced in	Coat length	Coat Colour	Fur Type
Non-pedigree shorthairs	Great Britain in 1880's	Short	Chocolate	Short, dense and firm

Cream British shorthair

Introduction: Cream British Shorthairs have been around for a long time now, but breeders still find it difficult to get the desirable shade of cream.

Appearance: Cream British Shorthairs are a very popular breed. They show red colouration or tabby markings but breeders have reduced tabby markings by selective breeding.

Behaviour: British Shorthairs love their food and they are the happiest if their food bowl is full and brimming. This justifies their size!

Factastic:
Did you know that because of its muscular, almost-square body, British Shorthairs have been nicknamed the bull dog of the cat family?

Ancestry	Introduced in	Coat length	Coat Colour	Fur Type
Non-pedigree shorthairs	Great Britain in 1880's	Short	Cream with red colouration	Short, dense and firm

Black Smoke British shorthair

Introduction: You must be wondering how does one differentiate between a Black Shorthair and a Black Smoke Shorthair? Simple - by the shimmer. Black Shorthairs don't shimmer whereas Black Smokes Shorthairs do.

Appearance: Now you may be wondering why do Black Smokes shimmer? It is because they have a silver undercoat and a black overcoat! The contrast gives the cat a shimmering effect.

Behaviour: Though the British Shorthairs mature slowly, they are not slow in making their way into your heart and home. They might wander outdoors for a while, but they like to come back to the cosy comfort of the house.

Factastic:
British Shorthairs are also called 'four feet on the ground' because they prefer to be patted rather than being picked up.

Ancestry	Introduced in	Coat length	Coat Colour	Fur Type
Non-pedigree shorthairs	Great Britain in 1880's	Short	Silver/White undercoat and black overcoat	Short, dense and firm

Red Classic Tabby British shorthair

Introduction: British Shorthairs have been found on the streets of Britain for a long time. Harrison Weir loved these cats so much that he bought some home and almost single-handedly created a new breed.

Appearance: The red markings are clearly defined and symmetrical as in the case of all tabbies. The butterfly wings on the shoulder and the rings on the legs make it a perfect red tabby.

Behaviour: British Shorthairs are very affectionate but they do not believe in showing it off. You will find your cat following you though it might not want to cuddle.

Factastic:
The word 'tabby' has the strangest origin – it is derived from Al Attabiya, a district in Baghdad, Iraq. The place is known for the black and white 'watered' silk it produced.

Ancestry	Introduced in	Coat length	Coat Colour	Fur Type
Non-pedigree shorthairs	Great Britain in 1880's	Short	Dark red tabby	Short, dense and firm

Red Mackerel Tabby British shorthair

Introduction: The only difference between a Classic Tabby and a Mackerel Tabby is the way the coat is patterned. Mackerel tabbies do not have the classic symmetrical swirls on their body like the Classic tabbies but they have the same red nose.

Appearance: Mackerel tabbies have a dark line that runs along their back and smaller lines that originate there and fall onto the sides of the body.

Behaviour: British Shorthairs are very hardy so you can keep them in most conditions. And they will be your companion for a long time as they have a lifespan of 15 – 18 years!

Factastic:
The Mackerel Tabby is so called because lines resembling a fish's skeleton run down the sides of its body. A 'Salmon Tabby' wouldn't have sounded quite right!

Ancestry	Introduced in	Coat length	Coat Colour	Fur Type
Non-pedigree shorthairs	Great Britain in 1880's	Short	Red tabby against paler body colour	Short, dense and firm

Colourpointed British shorthair

Introduction: Two beautiful cats – the British Shorthair and the Siamese – were brought together to produce the Colourpointed British Shorthair. They have the beautiful coat of the British Shorthair and the stunning points of the Siamese.

Appearance: Colourpointed British Shorthairs are found in various colours – cream point, blue point, seal point, red point, chocolate point, blue-cream point and seal tortie point etc.

Behaviour: Colourpoints are very affectionate cats. They not only love to show affection, they like to get a lot of it in return as well.

Factastic:
The Siamese has only four colours but the Colourpoint has twelve different colour points!

Ancestry	Introduced in	Coat length	Coat Colour	Fur Type
Non-pedigree shorthairs	Great Britain in 1980's	Short	Various	Short, dense and crisp

Blue Burmese

Introduction: People often get confused between a Burmese and a Malayan, but in reality they are the same thing. Some US registries consider only the sable brown coloured Burmese to be a true Burmese. Any other colour is called a Malayan cat.

Appearance: The gloss, considered a sign of good health, on a Burmese's coat is more obvious on the face, feet and ears. The back and tail generally have a darker shade of colour.

Behaviour: The Burmese is a very playful and affectionate breed and loves to follow its owner everywhere – sometimes to places one wouldn't be think possible!

Factastic:
The first Blue Burmese kitten was born by chance and was named Sealcoat Blue Surprise because everyone was surprised to see the blue colour.

Ancestry	Introduced in	Coat length	Coat Colour	Fur Type
Non-pedigree shorthairs	Thailand in 1400's	Short	Blue	Short, glossy, satin-like

Champagne Burmese

Introduction: The Burmese are muscular cats with heavy, velvety coats. Like the shorthairs, the Burmese males are larger than the females.

Appearance: Champagne Burmese are beautifully covered in a chocolate colour. The colour is spread evenly on the body with the face, tail and legs darker than the coat colour.

Behaviour: The Burmese are easily trainable. So easily that they can have and use their own scratching post. This means that the owner's furniture is safe from all those markings.

Factastic:
More popularly known as 'Chocolate' in Britain (for obvious reasons), these adorable cats were sent to Britain from the US in the later years of the 1960's.

Ancestry	Introduced in	Coat length	Coat Colour	Fur Type
Non-pedigree shorthairs	Thailand in 1400's	Short	Milk-chocolate	Short, glossy, satin-like

Cream Burmese

Introduction: A Red Tabby and a Blue Burmese were the parents of the first Cream Burmese in 1964. It took them six years to get recognised in Britain.

Appearance: Burmese kittens, especially Creams, generally are lighter coloured and show tabby markings. As they grow older, their coat colour darkens and they do not show tabby markings on any area other than the face.

Behaviour: Although you can leave your Burmese alone for a short time, it is not advisable to leave them alone for a long period. Loneliness can lead to behavioural problems which can make a Burmese very destructive.

Factastic:
Do not trying lifting up a Burmese for you may be in for a surprise. The Burmese is much heavier than it looks.

Ancestry	Introduced in	Coat length	Coat Colour	Fur Type
Non-pedigree shorthairs	Thailand in 1400's	Short	Cream	Short, glossy, satin-like

Red Burmese

Introduction: Burmese cats trace their origin to Wong Mau, the first cat transported to America from Burma in the 1930's. They have come a long way since then!

Appearance: Like the Cream Burmese, the Red Burmese also show some tabby markings on the face. The classic 'M' marking is conspicuously present on the forehead.

Behaviour: Burmese cats are as vocal as their Siamese ancestors, although their call is much sweeter. Burmese are known to call out to their owners when they want attention.

Factastic:
Did you know that the Burmese love to climb curtains and sit on doors? Imaging drawing the curtains and a ball of fur falling on you!

Ancestry	Introduced in	Coat length	Coat Colour	Fur Type
Non-pedigree shorthairs	Thailand in 1400's	Short	Light tangerine	Short, glossy, satin-like

Blue-gray Chartreux

Introduction: The origins of the breed are unknown, but it is widely believed that this breed was developed by the monks in the monastery of Le Grande Chartreuse in the 1300's.

Description: This muscular cat is popular for its fur type. The colour can vary between an ash to a slate-grey. The hairs are tipped with a silver which gives the coat a nice sheen.

Behaviour: Chartreux don't talk much, and some have been known to not talk at all! They are very relaxed and would rather observe than jump into action. This soft attitude makes them tolerant with strangers, children and other pets in the house.

Factastic:
Legend has it that the crusaders brought these cats back from the crusades and handed them over to monks to take care of the cats.

Ancestry	Introduced in	Coat length	Coat Colour	Fur Type
Non-pedigree shorthairs	1300's in France	Short	Bluish-gray with silver tips	Dense and glossy

Chausie

Introduction: Chausies are long and lean with a rectangular torso, deep chest and flat sides and can resemble cougars. Their legs are muscular and strong. Some Chausies are also seen with tufts on their ears.

Description: Chausies are a very healthy breed but some of them have been known to be gluten intolerant and to develop food allergies. Therefore, it is advised to follow a strict diet for Chausies.

Temperament: Chausies resemble a jungle cat but have a temperament of a domestic cat — affectionate, intelligent, good-natured and loyal. Chausies love to play around and are often seen busy with small toys.

Factastic:
Chausies are also known as Jungle Curls, the Mountain Cougars or the Stone Cougars.

Ancestry	Introduced in	Coat length	Coat Colour	Fur Type
Jungle cat and domestic cat	1960's, 1970's in France	Short	Brown ticked tabby, solid black, and black grizzled tabby	Soft and dense

Colourpoint shorthair

Introduction: Do not get confused between a Siamese and a Colourpoint Shorthair. In the US, the original four 'pure' colours – seal point, chocolate point, blue point and lilac point – are considered to be Siamese. Any other colour is considered a Colourpoint Shorthair.

Description: Siamese or Colourpoint Shorthairs can be identified even from a distance. The ends of the body – ears, face, legs and tail – are a darker colour than the base colour which is generally fawn or beige.

Behaviour: These cats are affectionate and loving. A Siamese will 'talk' to a wall if it can't find any other listener around!

Factastic:

Myth buster – contrary to popular belief, Siamese or Colourpoint Shorthairs are not mean! They will treat you the same way you treat them.

Ancestry	Introduced in	Coat length	Coat Colour	Fur Type
Non-pedigree Asiatics	1300's	Very short	Various	Fine, soft and glossy

Calico White Cornish Rex

Introduction: The Cornish Rex is so called because the first of its kind was born in Cornwall, England. Rex was added to their name to imply curly or otherwise unusual fur.

Description: Cornish Rexes have a slender, muscular body; large ears, oval-shaped eyes, long legs and a fine tail.

Behaviour: Cornish Rex's are very friendly, affectionate and loving cats. So much so that they are sometimes compared to dogs – because of the way they often follow their owner.

Factastic:
Do not take your Cornish Rex out for a walk in cold or rain because the lack of guard hairs makes it susceptible to the cold!

Ancestry	Introduced in	Coat length	Coat Colour	Fur Type
Non-pedigree shorthairs	1950 in Great Britain	Short	Any shade with patches of white	Soft, fine and curly

White Cornish Rex

Introduction: The first Cornish Rex was called Kallibunker and had very oriental looks. But pairing with Shorthairs has eventually made these cats slightly bigger.

Description: Cornish Rexes have no guard hairs or awn hairs. They just have down hairs which are very short. Their coat is incredibly soft – touching it feels like touching a rabbit's fur or a piece of velvet.

Behaviour: Since their fur is not very thick, these cats feel the cold easily. Therefore, you will always find them hanging around light bulbs, TV sets, computer monitors or other sources of heat.

Factastic:
Don't start looking for cheese if you smell cheese near your Cornish Rex – it's your cat! A peculiar scent gland in their paws gives them this odour.

Ancestry	Introduced in	Coat length	Coat Colour	Fur Type
Non-pedigree shorthairs	1950 in Great Britain	Short	White	Soft, fine and curly

Blue Smoke Cornish Rex

Introduction: Cornish Rexes have hard bodies, which are muscular, strong and very athletic. To add to this, they have long legs which make them a very tall breed.

Description: In Blue Smokes, the white gets hidden and the blue colour takes over. In this colour particularly, the ripples of the fur on the back and tail are very clear.

Behaviour: This breed is very intelligent and playful. They love playing games like fetch and many others – and if they run out of games, they might invent some of their own!

Factastic:

Do not overfeed your Cornish Rex because they have a tendency to put on weight. It not only spoils their look but is harmful too.

Ancestry	Introduced in	Coat length	Coat Colour	Fur Type
Non-pedigree shorthairs	1950 in Great Britain	Short	Blue	Soft, fine and curly

Red Smoke Cornish Rex

Introduction: The Cornish Rex has a small to medium build with an arched back. Coupled with a slender body, they often give the impression of being weak but that is far from reality!

Description: Red Smokes have a rich red colour 'smoke' on a lighter brown. This colour may not be too clear when the cat is sitting, but the 'smoking' effect is apparent when the cat is moving.

Behaviour: This breed is very fast, agile and attentive – it has all the qualities that make a good hunter.

Factastic:
Breeders tried to make a new variety of the Cornish Rex – one with long hair but it did not appeal to many cat fanciers.

Ancestry	Introduced in	Coat length	Coat Colour	Fur Type
Non-pedigree shorthairs	1950 in Great Britain	Short	Rich Red	Soft, fine and curly

Blue and White Cornish Rex

Introduction: There have been many Rex breeds that have come and gone but none were as popular as the Cornish Rex. The Cornish rex was recognised in 1967 and has been bred in many colours since.

Description: The Blue and White Cornish Rex has clear areas of blue and white. The blue is evenly spread on the body and the pattern is mostly symmetrical.

Behaviour: The Cornish Rex is an attention seeker – and will do anything to catch and hold your attention. They can be quite a handful, so beware.

Factastic:
The Cornish Rex is often seen wagging its tail like a dog to show pleasure and satisfaction. And when they are resting, they often curl the end of the tail.

Ancestry	Introduced in	Coat length	Coat Colour	Fur Type
Non-pedigree shorthairs	1950 in Great Britain	Short	Blue and White	Soft, fine and curly

Black Smoke and White Cornish Rex

Introduction: Markings are generally symmetrical in the Cornish Rex but some can be asymmetrical too. But asymmetry is not allowed in the Si-rex (Siamese-Rex).

Description: Black Smokes and White have a silvery undercoat which is clearly visible due to lack of guard hairs. The main colour is black with under parts, legs and a bit of the face in white.

Behaviour: The Cornish Rex loves to interact – with people and other animals. So you don't really need to worry if you have other pets or kids in the house.

Factastic:
The Cornish Rex has a very greasy tail due to the over secretion of the supracaudal organ at the base of the tail. It often leads to a condition called the 'Stud Tail'.

Ancestry	Introduced in	Coat length	Coat Colour	Fur Type
Non-pedigree shorthairs	1950 in Great Britain	Short	Black and White	Soft, fine and curly

Cymric

Introduction: There are three varieties of the Cymric – the Rumpy with no tail, the Stumpy with a stump for a tail and the Longy with a short tail.

Description: There are many colours and markings that are accepted in a Cymric (pronounced kim-ric). These cats are short and rounded and have an arched back.

Behaviour: The Cymric is a good-natured and friendly cat. It is very observant, playful, alert and intelligent.

Factastic:
The Cymric has a very unusual gait. It looks more like a rabbit when it is walking!

Ancestry	Introduced in	Coat length	Coat Colour	Fur Type
Long-haired Manx and Persians	1960's in Canada	Short	Various	Thick undercoat, glossy overcoat

Cream Lynx Point Si-rex Devon Rex

Factastic:
The Devon Rex is famously known as a 'monkey in a cat suit' because of the mischievous antics, such as the climbing and jumping it does!

Introduction: When the first set of Devon Rex kittens were born, they were thought to be Cornish Rex. But soon the breeders realised that though they looked similar, these had the overcoat as well as the undercoat.

Description: There are a lot of combinations – cream coloured with darker tabby markings and points! The tabby markings are particularly clear on the face and the tail.

Behaviour: The Devon Rex is a high jumper! It loves to climb the highest points in a room. So do not be surprised to find it on top of your curtains!

Ancestry	Introduced in	Coat length	Coat Colour	Fur Type
Non-pedigree shorthairs	1960 in Great Britain	Short	Pale cream with darker points	Soft, fine and velvety

Dilute Calico Devon Rex

Introduction: Often called 'Pixie Cat' or 'Alien Cat' because of their strange looks – large ears, large eyes, upturned nose, and small (or non-existent) whiskers!

Description: The Devon Rex loses a lot of hair while shedding which results in large areas of baldness. It is rarely permanent, so you don't need to worry.

Behaviour: The Devon Rex is not bothered about its surroundings but loves the people it is surrounded by. So if you want to be left alone, hard luck!

Factastic:
The Devon Rex is so called because it was first discovered in Buckfastleigh, Devon by Beryl Cox in 1960.

Ancestry	Introduced in	Coat length	Coat Colour	Fur Type
Non-pedigree shorthairs	1960 in Great Britain	Short	Pale cream with darker points	Soft, fine and velvety

Silver Torbie Devon Rex

Introduction: The Devon Rex is a very low maintenance cat. Shampooing, drying and nail trimming is all that your cat requires to be ready!

Description: Also known as 'patched tabbies' or 'tortie tabbies', torbies come in various patterns. In these cats, the black of a tortie is replaced by the tabby markings.

Behaviour: If your Devon Rex were a human, you would say it has OCD! This cat is obsessively compulsively attached to its owner and gives more than just loyalty and love.

Factastic:
Did you know that the Devon Rex makes friends not only with humans, but also with dogs and even parrots!

Ancestry	Introduced in	Coat length	Coat Colour	Fur Type
Non-pedigree shorthairs	1960 in Great Britain	Short	Pale cream with darker points	Soft, fine and velvety

Domestic shorthair

The Domestic Shorthair is the name given to any cat that neither belongs to a recognised breed nor is a pedigree. It is a result of generations of mixed breeding.

Description: Domestic Shorthairs are very healthy and do not need high maintenance. Being related to working cats does help.

Behaviour: These cats can vary greatly in temperament depending upon its parents.

Factastic:
Domestic Shorthairs love to eat and end up eating a lot! Therefore, make sure they play and exercise a lot.

Ancestry	Introduced in	Coat length	Coat Colour	Fur Type
Any	Unknown	Short	Various	Sleek and dense

Silver Egyptian Mau

Introduction: The original Egyptian Mau does not have a recorded history so nothing is known about them, but this new breed was developed by Princess Troubetskoy who obtained a cat with Egyptian Mau-like markings from Cairo and mated her with an Italian cat. The first two kittens were born in 1956.

Description: The Silver Egyptian Mau has black markings on a silver background. A dark line runs across its back and the tabby markings are distinct on the tail and forehead. It is a slender and muscular cat and is believed to be the one most responsible for the development of domestic cats.

Behaviour: Egyptian Maus are very intelligent, sensitive and responsive. And they are all the more responsive if they are around their owners.

Factastic:
The Egyptian Mau is the fastest breed of the domestic cats – it can run at a speed of 47 kph!

Ancestry	Introduced in	Coat length	Coat Colour	Fur Type
Non-pedigree shorthairs	1950's in Egypt	Short	Black spotting on silver	Fine, silky and dense

Black Smoke Egyptian Mau

Introduction: The Egyptian Mau is a spotted tabby shorthair. It is medium built – neither as cobby as the American shorthair nor as svelte as the Oriental breeds.

Description: The Egyptian Mau has a 'mascara' line which runs from the outer corner of the eye towards the side. It is almost joined by another one starting from the mid-cheek.

Behaviour: Egyptians Maus are very attentive and playful. They love to learn tricks to keep themselves busy. And if you want to fuss about them, they will be more than happy.

Factastic:
Egyptians are very food conscious and refrain from eating too much. They don't need to do much to maintain their figure!

Ancestry	Introduced in	Coat length	Coat Colour	Fur Type
Non-pedigree shorthairs	1950's in Egypt	Short	Smoked black	Fine, silky and dense

Black Silver Mackerel Tabby European shorthair

Introduction: All three kinds of markings – classic, mackerel and tabby – can be found on the European Shorthair. Although the body pattern depends on the type, the classic 'M' on the forehead is common to all.

Description: Silver with red markings, these cats have rings around the neck and a dark tail in addition to the mackerel tabby markings on the body.

Behaviour: European Shorthairs are very intelligent, independent, curious, agile and playful.

Factastic:
The European Shorthair was brought to Europe by Roman soldiers who used them to keep mice away from their food!

Ancestry	Introduced in	Coat length	Coat Colour	Fur Type
Non-pedigree shorthairs	1982 in Italy	Short	Black and silver	Short, crisp and very dense

Red Silver Mackerel Tabby European shorthair

Introduction: The Burmese cats trace their origin to Wong Mau, the first cat transported to America from Burma in the 1930's. They have come a long way since then!

Appearance: Like the Cream Burmese, the Red Burmese also show some tabby markings on the face. The classic 'M' marking is conspicuously present on the forehead.

Behaviour: The Burmese cats are as vocal as their Siamese ancestors, though their call is much cuter. Burmese are known to call out to their owners when they want attention.

Factastic:
Many European Shorthairs are called 'Bondkatt' in Swedish as they were bred on farms!

Ancestry	Introduced in	Coat length	Coat Colour	Fur Type
Non-pedigree shorthairs	1982 in Italy	Short	Red and silver	Short, crisp and very dense

Black Exotic shorthair

The Exotic Shorthair was developed by breeders in America who wanted their shorthairs to have Persian qualities. And what a wonderful job they did – Exotic Shorthairs are a wonderful variation of the Persian! They were recognised in 1967.

Description: Black Exotics are exotically black! Their colour is rich and thick and no other hues or markings can be seen on this cat. It is very important that these cats have perfect physical features as they don't have long hairs to hide any imperfections!

Behaviour: Exotic Shorthairs have inherited a good nature and social skills from the Persians, but are funnier and more inquisitive than them. They are always seen but rarely heard as they have a very soft voice.

Factastic:
These cats were named 'Exotic' to emphasize their connection to Persian cats. The first name considered for the breed was Sterling!

Ancestry	Introduced in	Coat length	Coat Colour	Fur Type
American Shorthair and Persian	1960's in USA	Short	Black	Soft and thick

Silver Torbie Exotic shorthair

Introduction: Barring the coat length, there isn't any other difference between Exotic Shorthairs and Persians. Like parents, like children.

Description: Both tabby and tortie markings are clearing visible in black on this cat with a silver base. They have a deep chest and broad shoulders.

Behaviour: These cats are very intelligent and sensitive. They respond to human emotions like very few others do. They can easily settle into your home at any age.

Factastic:
Exotic Shorthairs are lap cats – whether you like it or not! Forget your 'me' time if you have an Exotic Shorthair.

Ancestry	Introduced in	Coat length	Coat Colour	Fur Type
American Shorthair and Persian	1960's in USA	Short	Black and silver	Soft and thick

Havana Brown Oriental Shorthair

Introduction: Some of the early Siamese cats had a solid body colour and no coloured points. When they died out, breeders tried to recreate the type and hence the Oriental Shorthairs came about.

Description: The Havana Brown is the offspring of a Chocolate Point Siamese and a black non-pedigree cat. It is a slender cat with bright green eyes.

Behaviour: The Havana Brown has a soft voice but a very loud purr. It is known to attach to individuals, but the same can't be said for families.

Factastic:
This breed was known as the Chestnut Brown Foreign Shorthair until 1970. That is when it was renamed 'Havana'.

Ancestry	Introduced in	Coat length	Coat Colour	Fur Type
Siamese shorthairs	1950's in Great Britain	Short	Brown	Soft, glossy and very fine

Blue-point Himalayan

Introduction: Himalayans are very much like the Persian but for their blue-coloured eyes and coloured points. All Himalayan kittens are born with white fur. The colour begins to show only later and may take up to 18 months to show true potential.

Description: The Himalayans have a round body with short legs. They have prominent 'fur patch' which extends from the shoulders to between their legs. Himalayans have blue eyes and their pointed ends are blue coloured too.

Behaviour: Himalayans are sweet-tempered, good natured and social – so social that they will not think twice before jumping on the sofa and sitting between your friends. And as they have Siamese genes, they are very active too.

Factastic:
The Himalayan is known as the Colour Pointed Longhair in the US.

Ancestry	Introduced in	Coat length	Coat Colour	Fur Type
Persian and Siamese	1920's in USA	Long	White with blue colouration	Very fine, soft and thick

Japanese Bobtail

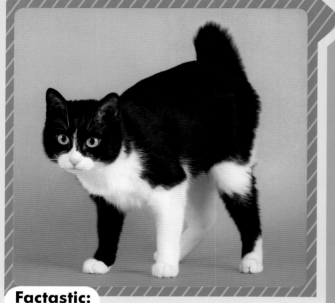

Introduction: The Japanese Bobtail has been around for more than a thousand years now. It's very popular in Japan and across southeast Asia but not so much in other parts of the world.

Description: The Japanese Bobtail is a small to medium sized cat known for its tail – or the absence of it! Its tail is barely four inches long and is almost inflexible. The tail is not cut or docked, but is naturally short.

Behaviour: Japanese Bobtails are very strong-willed, active and energetic. On the one hand it is easy to train the Japanese Bobtail to do things that it wants to do, and on the other hand, it is impossible to train it to not do things that it wants to do!

Factastic:
The Japanese Bobtail has nothing to do with the Manx. They are two different breeds and share nothing in common except a deformed tail.

Ancestry	Introduced in	Coat length	Coat Colour	Fur Type
Non-pedigree shorthairs	1000's in Japan	Short	Patterned black-red-white	Soft and silky

Blue Korat

Introduction: Korat is a province in Thailand and the cat has been so named because it has been around that area since first known. These cats are bluish-grey in colour and are one of the oldest stable cat breeds in the world.

Description: This cat has a medium-build, muscular body, but what is striking is its heart-shaped head and bright green eyes. This is one of the few breeds where there are no other colour options.

Behaviour: The Korat is an intelligent, intuitive and calm cat and will be happy to mingle with other pets until they know it is the boss! They love to bond with people as well.

Factastic:
Did you know that the Korat finds a mention in the Cat Book Poems of the Ayutthaya Kingdom which ruled between 1350 – 1767?

Ancestry	Introduced in	Coat length	Coat Colour	Fur Type
Unknown	1300–1700's in Thailand	Short	Blue	Fine and dense

Kurilian Bobtail

Introduction: These cats have been around for over 200 years around the islands of Sakhalin and Kuril and were brought to the Russian mainland in the 20th century. The shorthair is a natural breed but the longhair needs to be specifically bred.

Description: The Kurilian Bobtail is a well-built cat with strong bones and a tail that resembles pom-poms. It has a medium-to-large body with a rounded face. Kurileans, as they are also known, have a slightly arched back and their hind legs are longer than their front legs.

Behaviour: Kurilian Bobtails are not only brawny but also brainy. They love their territory and will examine and explore it from top to bottom!

Factastic:
Each Kurilian Bobtail has a 'special' tail that is unique to each cat. No two Kurilian Bobtails have the same tail!

Ancestry	Introduced in	Coat length	Coat Colour	Fur Type
Natural	1750-1850 in Sakhalin and Kuril Islands	Short or semi-long	Various	Soft and fine

LaPerm

Introduction: The LaPerm gets its name because its hair is curly, the curliest of them all being on the belly, throat and base of the ears – their whiskers are curly too. The LaPerm has a medium-to-long body with strong bones. It is a well-muscled breed and weighs between 8 to 10 pounds.

Description: LaPerms come in various colours and patterns and their fur is soft and curly which gives it a springy feel. It is a medium-sized, muscular cat with long legs and neck.

Behaviour: LaPerms are as inquisitive and intelligent as they are affectionate. They are known to make maximum use of their paws to get whatever they want!

Factastic:
LaPerm is so called because its fur is curly (perm) and not surprisingly, the first LaPerm kitten was called Curly!

Ancestry	Introduced in	Coat length	Coat Colour	Fur Type
Unknown	1982 in USA	Short	Various	Soft, curly and bouncy

Black Maine Coon

Introduction: The Maine Coon is one of the largest domestic cats and is the first longhaired breed that emerged on its own, without any assisted breeding! It has a distinctive physical appearance and has exceptional hunting skills.

Description: The Black Maine Coon is a stunning and imposing cat with a large bone structure and a rectangular body. It is black all over – the body, the paw pads, the nose and even the eye rims are black.

Behaviour: Maine Coons can adjust to any environment – indoors as well as outdoors. But they prefer a bit of both.

Factastic:
The Maine Coon is so called because it was first seen near Maine, on the east coast of America.

Ancestry	Introduced in	Coat length	Coat Colour	Fur Type
Non-pedigree Persian	1770's in USA	Long	Black	Thick, silky and of uneven length

White Maine Coon

Introduction: The Maine Coons are very heavy cats. Males can weigh up to 8 kg and females about the same! They sexes are evenly matched to each other.

Description: The White Maine Coon looks like a ball of white fur. It has such a huge body that even its rounded face looks small in comparison to the body.

Behaviour: These cats are very fond of their owners but they aren't too dependent on them. They like to be around but not fussed upon.

Factastic:
The Maine Coons have a very interesting fur style – the fur increases in length along the back.

Ancestry	Introduced in	Coat length	Coat Colour	Fur Type
Non-pedigree Persian	1770's in USA	Long	White	Thick, silky and of uneven length

Brown Classic Tabby Maine Coon

Introduction: The Maine Coon is a very hairy breed. It is so hairy that even its ears and paws are tufted.

Description: The base colour of the Brown Classic is a rich copper and it has black tabby marks spread all over it. The nose is a rich red in colour.

Behaviour: Maine Coons are relaxed and easy going in whatever they do – probably so even in a game of fetch with competition!

Factastic:
The Maine Coon length has a very long tail – it is as long as the length of the cat's back!

Ancestry	Introduced in	Coat length	Coat Colour	Fur Type
Non-pedigree Persian	1770's in USA	Long	Brown with black markings	Thick, silky and of uneven length

Brown Tabby and White Maine Coon

Introduction: The origin of the Maine Coon is unknown and as happens with most mysteries, there are various theories that circulate. The most popular being that when Mary Antoinette escaped France, she did so with six of her cats. She couldn't reach the US but her cats did – on the banks of Maine.

Description: True to its working ancestry, the Maine Coon has a strong, muscular body with broad chest and powerful legs. What makes this cat different from the Classic Tabby is the addition of white areas on the under parts and the feet.

Behaviour: Maine Coons are very playful. Males behave like clowns more often than not, but females are more poised. Both are equally affectionate – and it is difficult to say which is more so.

Factastic:
Legend has it that Maine Coons have descended from the longhaired cats that belonged to Marie Antoinette. They were sent to USA during the French Revolution for safety.

Ancestry	Introduced in	Coat length	Coat Colour	Fur Type
Non-pedigree Persian	1770's in USA	Long	Black	Thick, silky and of uneven length

Manx

Introduction: Rumpies (tailless Manx) are true Manx. There are specific genes in the cat which make them tailless. But not all Manx are tailless, in fact here are three other varieties with different tail lengths – Risers (just a bump in place of tail), Stumpies (a very short tail) and Longies (half to normal length tail).

Description: Rumpy Manx, the true Manx, has no tail but just a hollow where the tail would normally be. But the lack of a tail doesn't reduce their strength. They are as strong as all other forms.

Behaviour: The Manx is a very intelligent cat and is known to learn verbal commands better than many other cats. The Manx is a very skilful hunter and is often used by farmers whose fields are infested with rodents.

Factastic:
Many people believe that the first Manx cats swam to the Island of Man, off England's west coast in 1588 from a destroyed Spanish vessel.

Ancestry	Introduced in	Coat length	Coat Colour	Fur Type
Non-pedigree shorthairs	1600's in Great Britain	Short	Various	Dense and coarse

Munchkin

Introduction: The first Munchkin was sighted in the 1950's in Russia but disappeared for almost 30 years! The next one showed up in Louisiana in the 1980's.

Description: The Munchkins have abnormally short legs. It is a recessive gene that causes this abnormality, but short legs do not hamper their climbing or jumping abilities.

Behaviour: Munchkins are active, agile and extremely fast runners. They are very people oriented and love to be around them.

Factastic:
Munchkins are not a result of cross breeding. It is a gene that gives them short legs, much like Dachshunds! They were named Munchkins after the short people from the *Wizard of Oz*.

Ancestry	Introduced in	Coat length	Coat Colour	Fur Type
Natural	1950's in USA	Short	Various	Soft

Black and White Norwegian Forest

Norwegian Forest cats are known for their long, woolly, double-layered coats that are water repellent. Even heavy rain cant get through.

Description: The Black and White Norwegian Forest is a solidly built cat and has clearly marked black and white areas.

Behaviour: These are very smart and playful cats and love human company – they don't mind playing games with you.

Factastic:

In Norway, this cat is known as Norsk Skaukatt.

Ancestry	Introduced in	Coat length	Coat Colour	Fur Type
Angoras and Shorthairs	1520's in Norway	Semi-long	Black and white	Woolly and glossy

Black Smoke and White Norwegian Forest

Introduction: These cats look so much like Maine Coons that at first glance you could get confused. But Norwegian Forests are slightly smaller than Maine Coons.

Description: The smoke colouration is very defined in Black Smokes because of the thick white undercoat and dark colouration of the overcoat.

Behaviour: Norwegian Forests do not get stressed easily. So, if you have kids in the house, rest assured, your cat won't mind playing all day long.

Factastic:

Norwegian Forests are also called Wegies (wee-jees) and have a farm cat ancestry.

Ancestry	Introduced in	Coat length	Coat Colour	Fur Type
Angoras and Shorthairs	1520's in Norway	Semi-long	Black and white	Woolly and glossy

Silver Ocicat

Introduction: The Silver Ocicat is the offspring of a male Chocolate Point Siamese and a female that was a cross between an Abyssinian and a Seal Point Siamese.

Description: The Silver Ocicat has black spots, like a wild cat, on a silvery background. The lines around the neck and the legs are broken into spots too.

Behaviour: Although it looks wild and has certain wild cat characteristics, the Ocicat is in reality a 'pussy cat', very home bound and friendly.

Factastic:
Before it got this name, the Ocicat was known as Ocelette (for the similarity to an ocelot) and Accicat (because it was accidently bred). Ocicat is a combination of those two names.

Ancestry	Introduced in	Coat length	Coat Colour	Fur Type
Siamese and Siamese or Abyssinian	1964 in USA	Short	White with brown tabby markings	Lustrous and smooth

Ojos Azules

Introduction: The one thing that sets the Ojos Azules apart from other cats are their deep, blue eyes. This is a very rare breed and hasn't been recognised by any cat registry.

Description: These cats are medium sized with a triangular head, a proportionate tail and hind legs longer than the forelegs. There are said to have some neurological disorders due to odd genetic mutations.

Behaviour: Since it is a rare breed, nothing definite can be said about their temperament, but they are thought to be active, friendly and affectionate.

Factastic:
Ojos Azules means 'blue eyes' in Spanish, and this is why the cat is so called!

Ancestry	Introduced in	Coat length	Coat Colour	Fur Type
Unknown	1984 in USA	Short	Various	Soft, silky and glossy

Oriental Bicolour

Introduction: Any oriental cat with a huge area of white caused by genetics is known as a bicolour. The first Oriental Bicolour was born to a Siamese and a Bicolour American shorthair.

Description: the Oriental Bicolour is slender and long with a whip-like tail. Most of them have green eyes, except the colourpoints, which have blue eyes.

Behaviour: These are intelligent and curious cats. They will 'talk' to you in their own way and expect an answer too!

Factastic:
Oriental Bicolour as a breed was recognised by TICA in 1983.

Ancestry	Introduced in	Coat length	Coat Colour	Fur Type
American Bicolour Shorthair and Siamese	1970's in USA	Short or long	Various	Fine, silky and glossy

Blue Oriental shorthair

Introduction: Some of the first Siamese cats were ones without coloured points, but these died out early on. However people loved these cats so much that they decided to 'recreate' them. Attempts to recreate these cats led to the Oriental Shorthair.

Description: Blue Orientals are pure blue in colour with no white hairs. Like all Orientals, they have a long, triangular face and medium-sized, almond-shaped eyes. Their eyes are green without any flecks.

Behaviour: Oriental Shorthairs are a people cat. They love to be around people and are very talkative! It goes without saying that they hate to be alone just because they love to yap their time away.

Factastic:
Oriental Shorthairs are also called 'Ornamentals' because they can be bred in over 300 colours and patterns!

Ancestry	Introduced in	Coat length	Coat Colour	Fur Type
Siamese crosses	1950's in Great Britain	Short	Blue	Fine and glossy

Cinnamon Oriental shorthair

Introduction: The first Cinnamon Oriental was born in the 1960's to a Havana and a Sorrel Abyssinian in the Netherlands.

Description: The cinnamon colour is consistent from tip to base without any colouration and the green eyes slant towards the nose.

Behaviour: Orientals love their toys and each has a favourite, be it catnip sacks, rattle mice or just paper!

Factastic:
This breed is also known as an 'Oriental Caramel' in US and 'Blonde Havana' in the Netherlands.

Ancestry	Introduced in	Coat length	Coat Colour	Fur Type
Siamese crosses	1950's in The Netherlands and Great Britain	Short	Cinnamon brown	Fine and glossy

Red Oriental shorthair

Introduction: Oriental Shorthairs can be bred in self colour or any pattern. They are not only found in solid colours, but also in smoked patterns, shaded, parti-colour, tabby, and bicoloured varieties - almost 300 colours and patterns!

Description: Tabby markings are very common in Red Orientals, especially in kittens. Orientals have a long tail that is even at the base but tapers towards the end.

Behaviour: Even in Behaviour, Oriental Shorthairs are like the Siamese – friendly and affectionate. And they love hunting – so next time you spot a rat in the house, you know who will help.

Factastic:
In Great Britain, solid-coloured cats of this breed are called Foreign Shorthairs and only the marked ones, such as the Red Tabby, are called Oriental Shorthairs.

Ancestry	Introduced in	Coat length	Coat Colour	Fur Type
Siamese crosses	1950's in Great Britain	Short	Warm red	Fine and glossy

White Oriental shorthair

Introduction: Oriental Shorthairs are like the Siamese in many ways – they have the same lean slender body, long legs and large ears. With all these plus points, they are beautiful cats.

Description: White Orientals are a brilliant white colour and their eyes are sparkling blue. This means they need to be groomed on a regular basis to keep them spotlessly clean!

Behaviour: Orientals might look shy, but they have very strong and distinctive personalities. Don't be fooled by their looks! Shyness is one thing, and possessiveness is another. These are very possessive cats, which might make them seem obsessive and difficult!

Factastic:
Two of the three early White Orientals had a deafness problem (considering their blue eyes) but this issue has been eliminated now.

Ancestry	Introduced in	Coat length	Coat Colour	Fur Type
Siamese crosses	1950's in Great Britain	Short	White	Fine and glossy

Factastic:
These cats are known as Persians in the US and Persian Longhairs in the UK.

Blue-eyed White Persian

Introduction: Persians have been around since Victorian times but their appearance has changed since then. What has not changed is the fact that they are still deemed as regal and gorgeous as they were hundreds of years ago.

Description: Blue-eyed White Persians are strikingly beautiful! Blue eyes set against a cobby, muscular body with sparkling white fur add to their appearance and appeal.

Behaviour: Persians are not only beautiful looking but have a sweet and gentle nature as well. Once you bring them home, they will be around you forever.

Ancestry	Introduced in	Coat length	Coat Colour	Fur Type
Angoras and Persians	1880's in Great Britain	Long	White	Fine, thick and silky

Odd-eyed White Persian

Introduction: The 'original' White Persians were the Angoras who were found near Persia (now Iran) and Turkey. They were brought to Europe in the 1600's and to America only in the 1800's!

Description: As the name suggests, the Odd-eyed Persian has odd eyes – one orange or copper and one blue!

Behaviour: Persians are relaxed and easy going. They don't bother much and don't like to get bothered either.

Factastic:
Some Odd-eyed Persians are deaf, and the deafness occurs in the ear on the same side as the blue eye.

Ancestry	Introduced in	Coat length	Coat Colour	Fur Type
Angoras and Persians	1880's in Great Britain	Long	White	Fine, thick and silky

Orange-eyed White Persian

Introduction: The Orange-eyed Persian was developed by crossing Blue, Cream and Black Persians.

Description: Some kittens have a dark marking on their head which disappears when the kitten grows older.

Behaviour: Persians can be good and bad. They are good with friendly and decent children, but when they come across boisterous children, nobody can control them!

Factastic:
The Blue-eyed and the Orange-eyed were made two separate categories of the Persian cat in 1938.

Ancestry	Introduced in	Coat length	Coat Colour	Fur Type
Angoras and Persians	1880's in Great Britain	Long	White	Fine, thick and silky

Black Persian

Introduction: In comparison to their historic look, the Persian now has a more rounded face, smaller ears, and a thicker coat.

Description: Adults have a rich, black coat. Kittens sometimes have a bit of grey or a rusty hue, which goes when they are about eight months old.

Behaviour: Although Persians are not demanding at all, they need a stroke or cuddle at least once a day.

Factastic:
The black coat of this breed is said to be formed due to mutation in tabby coat genes!

Ancestry	Introduced in	Coat length	Coat Colour	Fur Type
Angoras and Persians	1880's in Great Britain	Long	Black	Fine, thick and silky

Blue Persian

Introduction: The first Blues were born by selectively breeding Black and White Persians and eliminating the white furs.

Description: Some Blue Persian kittens have tabby markings which disappear with age.

Behaviour: Persians are very focussed. So focussed that sometimes they develop a liking for only one person in a family!

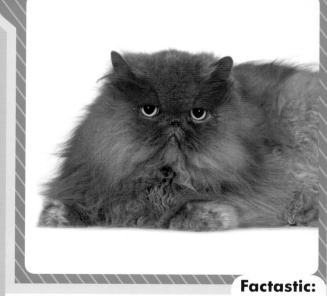

Factastic:
What's interesting is the fact that the Blue Persian with tabby markings turns out to be a most stunning looking adult!

Ancestry	Introduced in	Coat length	Coat Colour	Fur Type
Angoras and Persians	1880's in Great Britain	Long	Blue	Fine, thick and silky

Cream Persian

Introduction: Persians have long furs which can get matted very easily. They need to be combed at least once a day.

Description: A pale to medium shade of cream is the ideal colour a Cream Persian should be, and with no markings on the fur.

Behaviour: Persians adapt very well. So, whether it is a new pet, a newborn child or a new friend, Persians will always show them around!

Factastic:
If kept in good environment and given proper food and care, a Persian can live up to 20 years!

Ancestry	Introduced in	Coat length	Coat Colour	Fur Type
Angoras and Persians	1880's in Great Britain	Long	Light cream	Fine, thick and silky

Golden Persian

Introduction: Persian cats have a soft, melodious voice. So even if they keep meowing all day, you shouldn't mind too much.

Description: Golden Persians have an apricot background colour with chocolate or black tippings. Any other pattern on the body should be the same colour as the tipping.

Behaviour: Persians are very expressive, and they will use anything, even their eyes, to express emotions!

Factastic:
Did you know that the Persian has poor quality teeth, due to the flatness of the face!

Ancestry	Introduced in	Coat length	Coat Colour	Fur Type
Angoras and Persians	1880's in Great Britain	Long	Apricot with chocolate or black tippings	Fine, thick and silky

Red Persian

Introduction: The Red Persians are commonly known as Orange! Breeding a solid colour 'Orange' is sometimes difficult because of tabby cross-breedings in the past.

Description: Reds have a rich red colour with copper eyes. Kittens have tabby markings which generally disappear when the kitten grows older.

Behaviour: Persians don't mind living indoors. So, if you want to watch TV all day, they will be happy to keep you company.

Factastic:
Do you know how breeders overcame a shortage of female Red Persians? By crossing male Reds with torties!

Ancestry	Introduced in	Coat length	Coat Colour	Fur Type
Angoras and Persians	1880's in Great Britain	Long	Red	Fine, thick and silky

Black and White Persian

Introduction: The bicolour Persians are the same as solid coloured ones in body type, characteristics, temperament etc.

Description: Bicolours have a symmetrical pattern of markings. The most desirable have a white collar in the rich black back.

Behaviour: Persians in general are very sweet cats but once while, one odd cat can be born who would be so demanding and want to be treated like royalty!

Factastic:
The bicolours were called also 'magpies' for their resemblance to the bird!

Ancestry	Introduced in	Coat length	Coat Colour	Fur Type
Angoras and Persians	1880's in Great Britain	Long	White and black	Fine, thick and silky

Blue and White Persian

Introduction: Persians have round eyes set on a flat face. Their face is so flat that it looks like they have no nose!

Description: In Blue and Whites, there is a clear contrast of the two colours on the body as well as on the face.

Behaviour: Persians are very down to earth, literally! They like their feet on the ground so do not make great climbers and jumpers.

Factastic:
Did you know that the Persians were illegally smuggled out of Persia with spices, food and jewels? What exotic cats!

Ancestry	Introduced in	Coat length	Coat Colour	Fur Type
Angoras and Persians	1880's in Great Britain	Long	White and blue	Fine, thick and silky

Cream and White Persian

Introduction: Persians are not only the most popular, but also the most dignified and beautiful breed of cats.

Description: A pale cream and a pure white come together to make this bicolour. Colour division could be anywhere between half to one third.

Behaviour: Persians are posers – you might find them draped in your curtains adding beauty to your living room!

Factastic:
Do you know what is the love for cats called? It is called 'Ailurophilia'!

Ancestry	Introduced in	Coat length	Coat Colour	Fur Type
Angoras and Persians	1880's in Great Britain	Long	White and pale cream	Fine, thick and silky

Red and White Persian

Introduction: Red and Whites, are very difficult to breed for the same reason as pure reds – some cats may have tabby markings even when they mature.

Description: This cat has defined areas of pure white and rich red, and some areas of shading, which add to the beauty of the cat.

Behaviour: If your Persian's tail is quivering, it means it is showing love; but when it is thrashing, keep away!

Factastic:

Like humans have finger prints, cats have nose prints! These prints are unique to each individual.

Ancestry	Introduced in	Coat length	Coat Colour	Fur Type
Angoras and Persians	1880's in Great Britain	Long	White and rich red	Fine, thick and silky

Shaded Silver Persian

Introduction: it is very difficult to differentiate between Shaded Silvers and Chinchillas because the difference it only a matter of shade!

Description: These cats have black tippings on a striking silver background. Almost one third of each hair length should be coloured.

Behaviour: Persians, like many other cats, can read your moods and will respond accordingly.

Factastic:

The largest litter ever produced was that from a Persian named Bluebell. She produced 14 kittens in one litter!

Ancestry	Introduced in	Coat length	Coat Colour	Fur Type
Angoras and Persians	1880's in Great Britain	Long	White with dark black tips	Fine, thick and silky

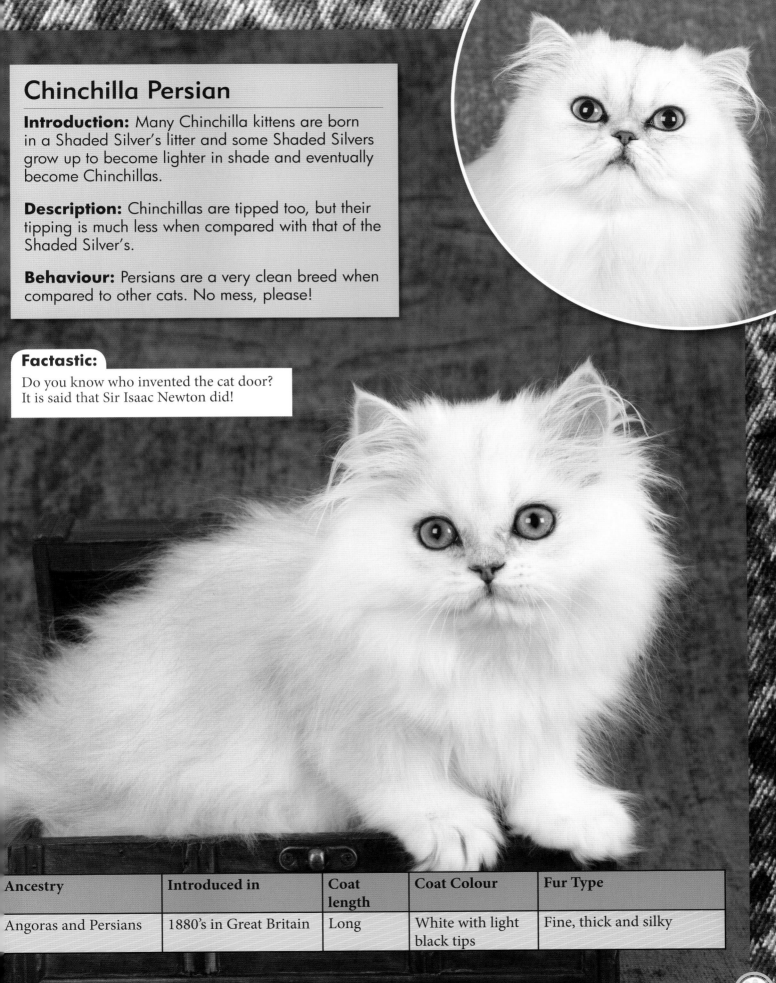

Chinchilla Persian

Introduction: Many Chinchilla kittens are born in a Shaded Silver's litter and some Shaded Silvers grow up to become lighter in shade and eventually become Chinchillas.

Description: Chinchillas are tipped too, but their tipping is much less when compared with that of the Shaded Silver's.

Behaviour: Persians are a very clean breed when compared to other cats. No mess, please!

Factastic:

Do you know who invented the cat door? It is said that Sir Isaac Newton did!

Ancestry	Introduced in	Coat length	Coat Colour	Fur Type
Angoras and Persians	1880's in Great Britain	Long	White with light black tips	Fine, thick and silky

Brown Classic Tabby Persian

Introduction: The Brown Tabby Persian Cat Society is one of the oldest specialist cat clubs in Britain.

Description: Rich sable with brown tabby markings make this variety 'classic'. Copper eyes and brick-red nose add to their beauty.

Behaviour: Your Persian has dreams too, just like you! So if you see your cat smiling with its eyes closed, you know it is probably dreaming of mice!

Factastic:
Tabbies have broken many records – Dusty, a Texas Tabby, produced 420 kittens in eighteen years!

Ancestry	Introduced in	Coat length	Coat Colour	Fur Type
Angoras and Persians	1880's in Great Britain	Long	Brown	Fine, thick and silky

Red Tabby Persian

Introduction: Red Tabbies were originally known as Orange Tabbies. Very popular in North America, their numbers have declined since World War II.

Description: Dark red tabby markings on a rich red background – a play of colours is what makes this variety special.

Behaviour: Like all the other cats, Persians, too, can see very well at night because they need only a sixth of the light that we need to be able to see.

Factastic:
Did you know that cats do not meow at other cats. They do it only to humans!

Ancestry	Introduced in	Coat length	Coat Colour	Fur Type
Angoras and Persians	1880's in Great Britain	Long	Red	Fine, thick and silky

Tortie Persian

Introduction: Tabby torties, or torbies, show clear markings of cream and red on a copper-brown background.

Description: As with all torties, torbies too are females. Their genetic makeup is such that males cannot be bred.

Behaviour: Persians, like most other cats, prefer their food at room temperature.

Factastic:
Now a tortie tabby record – Towser, a torbie, killed 28,899 mice in her lifetime! She lived for 21 years.

Ancestry	Introduced in	Coat length	Coat Colour	Fur Type
Angoras and Persians	1880's in Great Britain	Long	Brown, cream, red	Fine, thick and silky

Chocolate Tortie Persian

Introduction: The best time to see the true colour of a Chocolate Tortie is winter when the its coat is thick and the colour rich.

Description: Chocolate Torties have light and dark patches of chocolate on a lighter chocolate background.

Behaviour: Like all other cats, Persians will 'mark' other cats and humans with their scent glands. The ones near the temple area and the tail are the most common used.

Factastic:
Cats hate the smell of lemons and oranges – so if you want to save your favourite piece of furniture from being scratched, you know what to put there.

Ancestry	Introduced in	Coat length	Coat Colour	Fur Type
Angoras and Persians	1880's in Great Britain	Long	Chocolate	Fine, thick and silky

Black Smoke Persian

Introduction: Persians are high-maintenance cats. Their fur needs to be combed to prevent matting, and cleaned to reduce grease.

Description: This variety has white fur which is smoked black! They need to be groomed regularly to help the colours to stand out.

Behaviour: Persians are very obedient, and they will learn almost anything if you train them well.

Factastic:
A group of kittens is called a kindle and a group of grown cats is called a clowder.

Ancestry	Introduced in	Coat length	Coat Colour	Fur Type
Angoras and Persians	1880's in Great Britain	Long	Black and silver	Fine, thick and silky

Blue Cream Persian

Introduction: This variety has shades of blue and cream smoked on a stark-white background.

Description: Blue Creams have the classic facial blaze and the play of colours is most distinct across the head.

Behaviour: Persians are a favourite at cat shows, in TV commercials and other similar programmes because they are very well behaved.

Factastic:
Did you know that cats are the sleepiest of all mammals and can sleep for almost 16 hours a day!

Ancestry	Introduced in	Coat length	Coat Colour	Fur Type
Angoras and Persians	1880's in Great Britain	Long	Blue, cream and white	Fine, thick and silky

Tortoiseshell Persian

Introduction: The Tortie Persians were first developed in the 1890's and soon became very popular.

Description: This variety is a mix of four colours – black and brown background with patches of cream and red.

Behaviour: Tortie Persians are known for their delightful temperament. They are very friendly, placid and gentle.

Factastic:
Although Crookshanks, Hermione's cat (from Harry Potter) is probably a fictional species, it resembles a Persian cat!

Ancestry	Introduced in	Coat length	Coat Colour	Fur Type
Angoras and Persians	1890's in Great Britain	Long	Cream, red, black and brown	Fine, thick and silky

Silver Tabby Maine Coon

Introduction: Maine Coons take three to five years grow to their full size. And even if they mature physically, they remain 'kitten-like' all their life!

Description: The Silver Tabby has well-defined black markings on a silver background, but this is a very rare colour.

Behaviour: Maine Coons are good mothers though they produce very few kittens, just one litter a year.

Factastic:
The 'coon' of the Maine Coon probably comes from the fact that the striped tail of the cat resembles that of the racoon, or coon as they are known in North America.

Ancestry	Introduced in	Coat length	Coat Colour	Fur Type
Non-pedigree Persian	USA in 1770's	Long	Silver and black	Thick, silky and of uneven length

Calico Persian

Introduction: Calicos are known as 'Tortie and White' in Britain.

Description: Calicos have clear, defined areas of black, brown and white. Around one-third to half of the body is white with no shadings of other colours.

Behaviour: It is easy to train your Persian to use the litter box, but keep it clean otherwise your cat will not use it.

Factastic:

The Calicos are so called because their coat resembles the colourful cotton/cloth of the same name.

Ancestry	Introduced in	Coat length	Coat Colour	Fur Type
Angoras and Persians	1880's in Great Britain	Long	Black, brown and white	Fine, thick and silky

Diluted Calico Persian

Introduction: Diluted Calicos are the offspring of Blue-cream and White Persians. They have defined white areas, such as the lower part of the body and the belly.

Description: It is essential that whites remains in their normal defined areas and does not start to grow in areas normally blue-cream.

Behaviour: Do not tease a Persian, because no matter how sweet it looks, it doesn't take nicely to being teased!

Factastic:

Like humans, cats also are 'rightie' or 'leftie' – right-pawed or left-pawed – but around 40% are ambidextrous too!

Ancestry	Introduced in	Coat length	Coat Colour	Fur Type
Angoras and Persians	1880's in Great Britain	Long	Blue-cream and white	Fine, thick and silky

Calico Van Persian

Introduction: Calico Van, or the Harlequin, is the variant of Calicos bred by using the Turkish Van. Calico Vans are pure white with colour markings on the head, ears and tail.

Description: Calico Vans were initially bred in three colours – black, cream and red – but bicoloured cats are becoming very popular now.

Behaviour: Persians will make friends with other pets if they are friendly too. If not, your Persian will be frightened of them.

Factastic:

If your cat falls from a high place, don't worry because its inner ear canal (which controls the cat's sense of balance) will right it and help it to land on its feet!

Ancestry	Introduced in	Coat length	Coat Colour	Fur Type
Angoras and Persians	1880's in Great Britain	Long	Black, cream and red	Fine, thick and silky

Peterbald

Introduction: Peterbald, as the name suggests, is a bald variety of cats although some can have a very short coat. The first Peterbald was born to a Donskoy male and an Oriental Shorthair female.

Description: Peterbalds are slim, graceful and muscular. They have a recessive gene which makes them bald.

Behaviour: Peterbalds are sweet and gentle and enjoy the company of humans and other pets.

Factastic:

Cats love to play hide-and-seek! Next time you don't see your cat around, don't panic – look in the closet or under the chair!

Ancestry	Introduced in	Coat length	Coat Colour	Fur Type
Donskoy and Oriental shorthair	1994 in Russia	Short or no hair	All colours and markings	Soft (ones with coat)

Pixie-bob

Introduction: Pixie-bobs have Bobcat ancestry and are bred to resemble North American Bobcats.

Description: Pixie-bobs are medium-sized cats which can be no-tailed, short-tailed or long-tailed. And they can have up to seven toes on their front paws!

Behaviour: Pixie-bobs are known for their chirps, chatters or growls. They aren't well known for their meowing, and some don't meow at all!

Factastic:

In cat competitions, Pixie-bob is the only polydactyl cat that is allowed. Any other polydactyl cat is disqualified.

Ancestry	Introduced in	Coat length	Coat Colour	Fur Type
Bobcat	1986 in USA	Short or long	All colours and patterns	Fine and soft

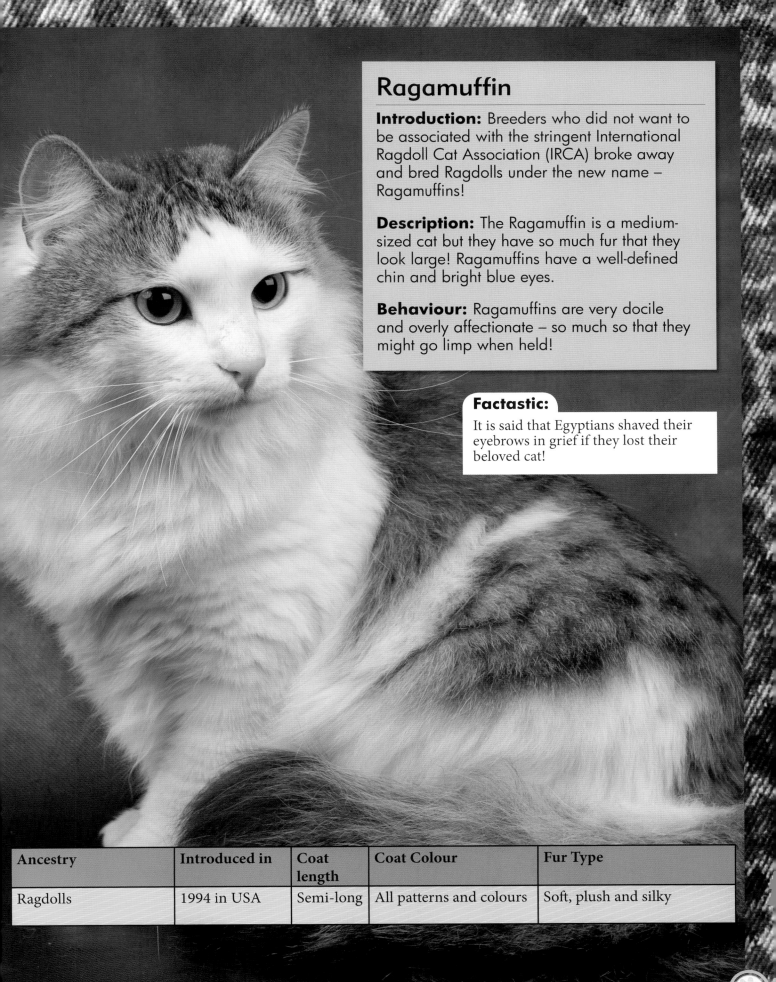

Ragamuffin

Introduction: Breeders who did not want to be associated with the stringent International Ragdoll Cat Association (IRCA) broke away and bred Ragdolls under the new name – Ragamuffins!

Description: The Ragamuffin is a medium-sized cat but they have so much fur that they look large! Ragamuffins have a well-defined chin and bright blue eyes.

Behaviour: Ragamuffins are very docile and overly affectionate – so much so that they might go limp when held!

Factastic:

It is said that Egyptians shaved their eyebrows in grief if they lost their beloved cat!

Ancestry	Introduced in	Coat length	Coat Colour	Fur Type
Ragdolls	1994 in USA	Semi-long	All patterns and colours	Soft, plush and silky

Blue Mitted Ragdoll

Introduction: Ragdolls come in various colours and generally three patterns – colourpointed, mitted and bicolour. Lynx can also be achieved by adding tabby markings to any of the three patterns.

Description: These are white cats with blue points – head, tail and legs. They are known for their white 'mittens' on their front paws and white socks on the back paws!

Behaviour: Ragdolls are very sweet, gentle and loving and will wow you with their good nature.

Factastic:
Legend has it that Noah was worried that rats would eat all the grain on his Ark and he prayed to God for help. God made a lion sneeze, and out came a cat!

Ancestry	Introduced in	Coat length	Coat Colour	Fur Type
Non-pedigree cats	1960's in USA	Semi-long	Blue-grey and white	Silky and dense

Seal Point Ragdoll

Introduction: Seal Point Ragdoll is an example of Colourpointed Ragdolls. They have longer hair on the neck giving it a bib-like look.

Description: Seal Points have shades of brown on a cream background. There are marked areas of beige too on the chest and belly.

Behaviour: Ragdolls are actually a like a child's doll if held. Like the Ragamuffin, they too, tend to go limp if held and stroked.

Factastic:
Ragdoll's are called 'gentle giants'! You can't get nicer cats than these – they are good companions!

Ancestry	Introduced in	Coat length	Coat Colour	Fur Type
Non-pedigree cats	1960's in USA	Semi-long	Cream, beige and seal-brown	Silky and dense

Seal Bicolour Ragdoll

Introduction: Ragdolls are large cats and take almost three years to grow to their full potential. All Ragdolls have blue eyes.

Description: In Seal Bicolours, a bit of white is allowed but the white should not extend to the brown points.

Behaviour: Ragdolls are not made for the outside world and are strictly an indoor breed. They are so gentle that they probably can't survive alone outside!

Factastic:

In order to maintain their unique style and pattern, Ragdolls are mated only to other ragdolls!

Ancestry	Introduced in	Coat length	Coat Colour	Fur Type
Non-pedigree cats	1960's in USA	Semi-long	White and seal-brown	Silky and dense

Russian shorthair

Introduction: Russian shorthairs are of a solid blue colour and no white or tabby markings are allowed in their breeding.

Description: The Blue has a silvery sheen on the coat. Even the nose and paw pads are blue! The only different colour on the body is in the eyes – which are green!

Behaviour: Intelligent and affectionate, Russian shorthairs are very easily trained.

Factastic:

Russian Shorthairs were known as Archangel Blues after the port from which they were brought into Britain.

Ancestry	Introduced in	Coat length	Coat Colour	Fur Type
Non-pedigree cats	1800's in Russia	Short	Black, blue and white	Fine and silky

Blue-cream and White Scottish fold

Introduction: The first Scottish Fold, later named Susie, appeared in a litter born to a farm cat. Susie's ears were folded.

Description: The ears are folded forward but because the flap looks down, the ears look folded towards the nose.

Behaviour: Scottish Folds are very sweet natured and are often seen 'supervising' whatever their owners are doing!

Factastic:

Scottish Folds love to sleep flat on their backs and very often you will also see them sitting upright, just like an otter!

Ancestry	Introduced in	Coat length	Coat Colour	Fur Type
Non-pedigree cats	1951 in Scotland	Short or long	Blue-cream and white	Dense and resilient

Black and White Scottish fold

Introduction: When Susie gave birth to another kitten with folded ears, William Ross, a local shepherd, decided to establish a new breed using that kitten.

Description: Black and white areas are defined, and when seen in bright sunlight, brownish hues can be seen on some black parts.

Behaviour: Scottish Folds like to play but would prefer it if their owners were a part of the game too.

Factastic:

Susie's folded-ear kitten was called Snooks.

Ancestry	Introduced in	Coat length	Coat Colour	Fur Type
Non-pedigree shorthairs	1951 in Scotland	Short	Black and white	Dense and resilient

Calico Scottish fold

Introduction: Scottish Folds come in many colours and patterns as breeding them is not difficult – only one Scottish Fold parent is needed to produce an offspring with similar characteristics.

Description: Another prominent feature of the Scottish Folds are the short and sturdy legs. If you see one, note carefully, just how short the legs are.

Behaviour: Scottish Folds are not very talkative and tend to save their voice for special occasions.

Factastic:
Kittens of any Scottish Fold litter have normal ears. Only after two to three weeks do the new Scottish Folds emerge out of the litter.

Ancestry	Introduced in	Coat length	Coat Colour	Fur Type
Non-pedigree shorthairs	1951 in Scotland	Short	White, brown and black	Dense and resilient

Selkirk Rex

Introduction: The first Selkirk Rex was born without any specialised breeding, to two non-pedigreed kittens. That kitten was later mated with a Black Persian to develop the breed of Selkirk Rex.

Description: These cats have curly fur which is their most prominent feature. Colour and pattern can vary but the eye colour should match the coat colour.

Behaviour: Selkirk Rexes are very tolerant, patient and loving, and will behave in a similar way to the way they are treated.

Factastic:
Not only the hairs on the body, the Selkirk Rex's whiskers are curly too!

Ancestry	Introduced in	Coat length	Coat Colour	Fur Type
Non-pedigree cat and Black Persian	1987 in USA	Short or long	Many colours and patterns	Curly, thick and plush

Serengeti

Introduction: Born to Oriental Shorthairs and Bengal cats, the Serengeti is a tall, medium-boned domestic cat.

Description: The Serengeti has very large, round ears placed directly over the skull and large, round, expressive eyes.

Behaviour: Serengetis take time to settle in new surroundings and may take some months to relax, but once they have, they may follow you everywhere!

Factastic:
The Serengeti was bred to resemble the Serval but has no Serval genes!

Ancestry	Introduced in	Coat length	Coat Colour	Fur Type
Oriental shorthairs and Bengal	1994 in USA	Short	Gold/Grey/Silver with black spots, solid black	Thick and soft

Serval

Introduction: The Serval, also known as the tiger-forest-cat is a very beautiful and elegant cat. It has a long, slender body and a short tail with black rings.

Description: This cat has pale yellow fur with black markings. It has either large black spots or several small spots. These spots merge into the longitudinal stripes on the back and neck.

Behaviour: The Serval is a nocturnal animal but some can be diurnal too. It has a very distinct 'chirp' that sounds like 'how-how-how'!

Factastic:
The Serval has the longest legs of any cat, thanks to the elongated metatarsal bones in its feet.

Ancestry	Introduced in	Coat length	Coat Colour	Fur Type
Natural	1990's in Africa	Short	Pale yellow with black markings	Fine

Cream Lynx Point Siamese

Introduction: Thanks to their attractive colours, Lynx Points were known as Silver Point Siamese and Attabiya before Lynx Point was accepted as their name.

Description: Cream Lynx Points are a mix of white and cream. The body is white, with upper parts and points in a pale cream colour.

Behaviour: Siamese are attention seekers and prove to be good company in households with many people.

Factastic:
Nemo, British Prime Minister Harry Wilson's pet, was a Siamese cat.

Ancestry	Introduced in	Coat length	Coat Colour	Fur Type
Non-pedigree Asiatics	Thailand in 1300's	Short	White and cream	Fine and glossy

Blue Point Siamese

Introduction: Blue Points are one of the oldest forms of the Siamese. They gained prominence around the 1930's and have retained that ever since.

Description: Blue Points have a white body with light blue colouration and dark blue points.

Behaviour: Extremely temperamental, the Siamese are the most friendly and affectionate of all cat breeds.

Factastic:
The Siamese get their name from 'Siam', the old name of Thailand.

Ancestry	Introduced in	Coat length	Coat Colour	Fur Type
Non-pedigree Asiatics	Thailand in 1300's	Short	White and blue	Fine and glossay

Lilac Point Siamese

Introduction: The Lilac Points have a white body with pinkish grey points. Good Lilac Points should not have any colouration.

Description: Lilac Points have large ears which are quite distinct. Their tail has very light ringing.

Behaviour: Siamese are very vocal and communicative, and though you might not understand them, they may understand you.

Factastic:
The first Lilac Point was disqualified from a cat competition as apparently it wasn't a good blue!

Ancestry	Introduced in	Coat length	Coat Colour	Fur Type
Non-pedigree Asiatics	Thailand in 1300's	Short	White and pinkish-grey	Fine and glossy

Seal Point Siamese

Introduction: Siamese are one of the few breeds that mature very quickly.

Description: This is the traditional colour of the Siamese. The points of this cat are seal brown with brown colouration on the body.

Behaviour: Siamese modulate their voice very smartly — when they are happy, they are soft, but when they are unhappy, they are not.

Factastic:

Siamese are known for their voice which can sound like that of a wailing child.

Ancestry	Introduced in	Coat length	Coat Colour	Fur Type
Non-pedigree Asiatics	Thailand in 1300's	Short	White and seal brown	Fine and glossy

Blue Lynx Point Siamese

Introduction: The Siamese cats were first described in 1793 by German explorer Peter Simon Pallas.

Description: Blue Lynx have points and shades of blue-grey broken by white bands.

Behaviour: Siamese are very playful, active and agile.

Factastic:

The Siamese are the most popular shorthaired cat breed in the US as declared by the Cat Fanciers' Association.

Ancestry	Introduced in	Coat length	Coat Colour	Fur Type
Non-pedigree Asiatics	Thailand in 1300's	Short	White and blue	Fine and glossy

Brown Spotted and White Siberian

Introduction: These cats have been around for so many years that no one is certain of their origins. It is believed that they are the ancestors of some long-haired breeds.

Description: Tabby markings are very clear on this cat because of their wild cat genes. They have a thick, water-repellent coat.

Behaviour: Siberian cats are often called 'dog-like' because they are loyal, affectionate and playful.

Factastic:

Harrison Weir described a Russian cat similar to the Siberian in his book *Our Cats and All About Them*.

Ancestry	Introduced in	Coat length	Coat Colour	Fur Type
Non-pedigree long-haired cats	Russia in 1000's	Long	White, brown and black	Glossy and dense

Sepia Agouti Singapura

Introduction: Singapuras are very sweet-looking and cute cats. They were first exhibited in the US in 1975.

Description: The Singapuras are very small cats with distinct pointed ears. Their underparts are lighter than the other parts of the body.

Behaviour: As sweet as they look, is as sweet they actually are. Singapuras are very even-tempered, calm cats.

Factastic:

These cats get their name from the Malaysian name for Singapore. Their ancestors were known as 'Drain Cats of Singapore'.

Ancestry	Introduced in	Coat length	Coat Colour	Fur Type
Non-pedigree long-haired cats	Singapore in 1965	Short	White and cream	Sleek and silky

Skookum

Introduction: Born to a Munchkin and a LaPerm, Skookum is a dwarf cat whose hind legs are noticeably longer than the forelegs.

Description: Skookums have a cobby body and curly hair like LaPerms. They have large, expressive eyes.

Behaviour: Despite their short stature, Skookums are very agile and athletic. They love to jump and climb.

Factastic:
Many Skookums are known to have dental problems. Even toothless, they would look beautiful, wouldn't they?

Ancestry	Introduced in	Coat length	Coat Colour	Fur Type
Munchkin and LaPerm	USA in 1990's	Short	Many	Soft and fuzzy

Seal and White Point Snowshoe

Introduction: This muscular, large breed was developed by Dorothy Hinds-Daugherty in Philadelphia.

Description: These cats can have white bodies with brown-coloured points or they could also show some shading on the body.

Behaviour: Snowshoes are gentle, loving and affectionate cats.

Factastic:
Snowshoes have white paws – that's why they are called 'Snowshoe' – and are like the Birmans but they do not have Birman ancestry.

Ancestry	Introduced in	Coat length	Coat Colour	Fur Type
Siamese and American shorthair	USA in 1960's	Short	White and seal brown	Fine and glossy

Blue Silver Somali

Introduction: Long-haired Somalis have been a part of Abyssinian litters for a very long time but were noticed for development only in 1967.

Description: The base colour is white and each hair is ticked with blue giving the body a rich, silvery shine.

Behaviour: Somalis are active and playful and have to be kept busy. They should be given enough toys to keep them amused.

Factastic:
Somalis were unwelcome in the beginning because it was thought they were a mistake caused by a recessive gene in the Abyssinian.

Ancestry	Introduced in	Coat length	Coat Colour	Fur Type
Long-haired Abyssinians	USA in 1967	Long	White and blue	Fine and soft

Chocolate Silver Somali

Introduction: The Somalis get their name from the country of Somalia, Ethiopia's (once known as Abyssinia) neighbouring country. So the choice of name is obvious!

Description: White with warm chocolate tickings give these cats a very soft feel. Like all Somalis, they have longer fur on their hind legs.

Behaviour: Somalis like company and are the happiest if they have another cat friend to play with.

Factastic:
The good things about Somalis is that they don't keep shedding throughout the year – they shed all at once, twice a year.

Ancestry	Introduced in	Coat length	Coat Colour	Fur Type
Long-haired Abyssinians	USA in 1967	Long	White and chocolate	Fine and soft

Sorrel Silver Somali

Introduction: Somalis are medium-sized, muscular cats. They have a curved profile and their pricked, tufted ears are distinctive.

Description: Like all silvers, the base colour is white, with sorrel tickings. Ears and tails are ticked too and the coloured tufting is visible between the toes as well.

Behaviour: Somalis are even-tempered and gentle and are suitable for households with children and other pets.

Factastic:
Do not trying lifting up a Burmese as you may be in for a surprise. The Burmese is much heavier than it looks. Remember, looks are very deceptive.

Ancestry	Introduced in	Coat length	Coat Colour	Fur Type
Long-haired Abyssinians	USA in 1967	Long	White and sorrel	Fine and soft

Sorrel Somali

Introduction: The coat of the Somalis is double layered. Also each hair has at least three bands of ticking.

Description: Their colour is a nice, warm red which is ticked with chocolate brown. Their ears are also ticked chocolate brown.

Behaviour: Somalis are very inquisitive by nature and will leave your cupboard in a mess if you leave it open by mistake!

Factastic:
If Somalis could choose a profession, it would be that of a hairdresser – some Somalis love to play with their owner's hair!

Ancestry	Introduced in	Coat length	Coat Colour	Fur Type
Long-haired Abyssinians	USA in 1967	Long	White and seal brown	Fine and soft

Black and White Sphynx

Introduction: The first Sphynx was born to a Black and White cat but now this cat is available in various colours and patterns. The Sphynx has a remarkably long tail.

Description: Though the tall and slender Sphynx is known to be a totally hairless breed, some hair can be seen on the extremes of the body.

Behaviour: The Sphynx is a very affectionate cat and will put in every effort to show you its love.

Factastic:

The Sphynx has very large and big ears which can look like a huge moth has been placed on the cat's head!

Ancestry	Introduced in	Coat length	Coat Colour	Fur Type
Non-pedigree shorthairs	Canada in 1966	Bald	Brown and white	Soft

Thai

Introduction: Thais are actually the Old-style Siamese and were given this new name in the 1990's.

Description: The Thais are known for their unique head shape. The rounded head has a distinct long and flat forehead and a wedge-shaped muzzle.

Behaviour: Thais are chatterboxes and known to 'yip and yap' with their owners!

Factastic:

Thais are said to have a great sense of humour – a joke anybody?

Ancestry	Introduced in	Coat length	Coat Colour	Fur Type
Natural	Thailand in 1990's	Short	Any coloured point	Fine and soft

Honey Mink Tonkinese

Introduction: Born to a Burmese and a Siamese, these cats were first known as Golden Siamese, as they had the rich golden colour of the Burmese and the pointing of the Siamese.

Description: Honey Minks have a light cream coloured coat with shadings of darker cream. They have a lithe, muscular body.

Behaviour: The Tonkinese is known to be very active and affectionate.

Factastic:

All the recognised colours of the Tonkinese cat are called 'Mink' in the US.

Ancestry	Introduced in	Coat length	Coat Colour	Fur Type
Burmese and Siamese	Burma in 1930's	Short	Cream	Fine and soft

Toyger

Introduction: The Toyger is a designer cat. In today's fast paced world where everything is custom-made, why not cats!? It was 'made' to resemble the tiger.

Description: The Toyger has a unique coat – broken black stripes in random order on a gold background.

Behaviour: Toygers are very intelligent and trainable. You can train them to walk on a leash and play fetch.

Factastic:

Toygers are so called because they look like toy tigers!

Ancestry	Introduced in	Coat length	Coat Colour	Fur Type
Shorthair tabbies	USA in 1980	Short	Gold and black	Fine and soft

Black Turkish Angora

Introduction: Turkish Angoras have been known in Europe since the 1600's and contributed in the development of the longhaired Turkish Angora.

Description: The best blacks have a dense coat of black with no shade of brown or white on their hairs. Their coat becomes shorter during the summer months.

Behaviour: Turkish Angoras are very inquisitive by nature, so much so that they might get locked in a cupboard without the owner knowing that their cat is investigating there!

Factastic:
Did you know that breeders used the Turkish Angoras almost to extinction, to improve the coat of the Persian breed?

Ancestry	Introduced in	Coat length	Coat Colour	Fur Type
Non-pedigree Persians	Turkey in 1400's	Long	Black	Fine and silky

White Turkish Angora

Introduction: When the Turkish Angora population became scarce, the Turkish government set up a breeding programme in Ankara Zoo in the 1960's to revive the breed.

Description: The original White is the one with odd eyes, two different colours, known as Ankara kedi. In fact, white is the original colour of the breed and it is this cat that was originally known as the Angora.

Behaviour: Turkish Angoras are very intelligent and energetic. They can play for hours at a stretch without getting tired.

Factastic:
The Turkish Angoras were recognised by the Cat Fanciers' Association in 1973 but until 1978, only white Angoras were recognised!

Ancestry	Introduced in	Coat length	Coat Colour	Fur Type
Non-pedigree Persians	Turkey in 1400's	Long	White	Fine and silky

Blue Mackerel Tabby Turkish Angora

Introduction: The Turkish Angora is one of the oldest surviving cat breeds in the world.

Description: These cats have a light blue body coloured with darker blue tabby markings. The thin lines running from the spine to the sides of the body add to their beauty.

Behaviour: Turkish Angoras are very vocal cats and are known to have lengthy 'conversations' with their owners!

Factastic:

Have you read *Felidae*? Do you remember the character of Felicity? Felicity was a Turkish cat.

Ancestry	Introduced in	Coat length	Coat Colour	Fur Type
Non-pedigree Persians	Turkey in 1400's	Long	Black	Light and dark blue

Auburn Turkish Van

Introduction: Turkish Cats have a distinct chalky-white colour and good Vans have other colours restricted to their head and tail. But some cats do have hints of colour in other areas.

Description: Auburns have defined areas set for colour – just above the eyes, not extending beyond the ears and the tail.

Behaviour: Turkish Vans are very agile and large cats. Their physical strength mirrors their mental ability.

Factastic:
Turkish Vans have long coats but did you know that their coats don't mat, which means very little grooming is required!

Ancestry	Introduced in	Coat length	Coat Colour	Fur Type
Non-pedigree local cats	Turkey in 1600's	Semi-long	White and auburn	Soft and silky

Cream Turkish Van

Introduction: The length of a Van's coat varies throughout the year. The coat is shorter during the summer and thicker during winter to keep warm.

Description: Cream Turkish Vans have a bit of cream on the head and a bit on the tail that may extend on to the back.

Behaviour: The Turkish Van loves to swim! Not only that, it loves to play in the water too. That's why it got it the name 'Swimming Cat'.

Factastic:
The Turkish Van is a rare and ancient breed that was developed in southwest Asia and is a national treasure in its homeland.

Ancestry	Introduced in	Coat length	Coat Colour	Fur Type
Non-pedigree local cats	Turkey in 1600's	Semi-long	White and cream	Soft and silky

Turkish Van Kedisi

Introduction: Turkish Vankedisi is a medium-sized cat with very muscular legs and a long and fluffy tail!

Description: Vankedisis are always white. They may have either blue or amber eyes or both. Odd-eyed Vankedisis are very valued.

Behaviour: Vankedisis are very energetic, so much so that they are known as terrible house pets because they might break a thing or two whilst trying to exhaust their energy!

Factastic:

Van kedisis are deaf!

Ancestry	Introduced in	Coat length	Coat Colour	Fur Type
Non-pedigree local cats	Turkey in 1600's	Long	White	Soft and silky

Ruddy Somali

Introduction: Ruddy Somalis are the oldest known of the Somalis and are often called 'Usual'.

Description: Ruddys have rich golden brown base colour ticked with black. The tickings are most visible on the spine and tail.

Behaviour: Somalis are very people oriented and would probably enjoy a party more than any person invited.

Factastic:

Thanks to the bushy tail and the ruddy coat, these cats are also known as fox cats!

Ancestry	Introduced in	Coat length	Coat Colour	Fur Type
Long-haired Abyssinians	USA in 1967	Long	Brown and black	Fine and soft

Black American Bombay

Introduction: Obvious from their look, the Black American Bombay was bred to create a 'black panther' of domestic cats. Though the breed is recognised in the US, it has not been recognised globally yet.

Description: A strong, oval body, dense black coat and brightly coloured eyes are distinctive features of the Black American Bombay. The original tabby pattern is visible in the coat of some cats. They have a medium tapering tail with no kinks.

Behaviour: Black American Bombays crave attention. They are very intelligent and friendly and are known to easily befriend kids because of which they are preferred to be kept as pets.

Factastic:
Black American Bombays are not born with the brightly coloured eyes that they are known for. The colours of their eyes at birth is blue which later changes to grey and finally to the desired gold/copper colour.

Ancestry	Introduced in	Coat length	Coat Colour	Fur Type
Burmese and American Shorthair	United States of America in 1950's	Short	Black	Shiny, short and sleek

Black-tipped British shorthair

Introduction: Black-tipped British Shorthairs got their name in 1978 but that doesn't mean that the breed is quite young. Before that, they were known as Chinchilla Shorthairs.

Description: These cats have pure white fur with black ends, but this colouration appears only on the upper and side parts of the body. The under parts of the body are just pure white.

Behaviour: British Shorthairs are very good natured and intelligent. That's the reason they are a favourite with animal trainers. Who doesn't like a trainee who listens?

Factastic:
Black-tipped British Shorthairs are Hollywood figures! They have appeared in many movies and TV commercials. Their intelligence gets them these roles!

Ancestry	Introduced in	Coat length	Coat Colour	Fur Type
Non-pedigree shorthairs	Great Britain in 1880's	Short	White furs with black ends	Short, dense and firm

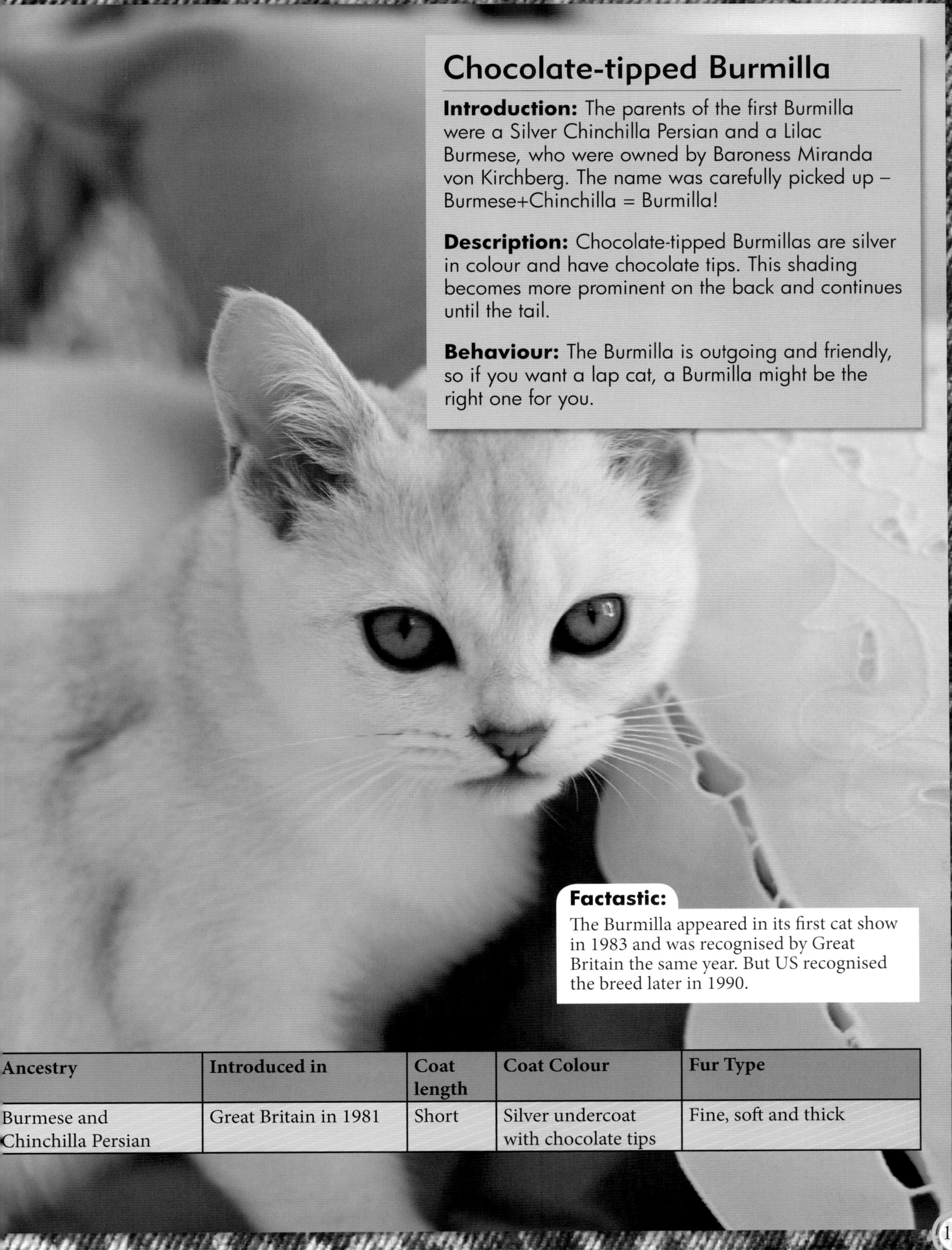

Chocolate-tipped Burmilla

Introduction: The parents of the first Burmilla were a Silver Chinchilla Persian and a Lilac Burmese, who were owned by Baroness Miranda von Kirchberg. The name was carefully picked up – Burmese+Chinchilla = Burmilla!

Description: Chocolate-tipped Burmillas are silver in colour and have chocolate tips. This shading becomes more prominent on the back and continues until the tail.

Behaviour: The Burmilla is outgoing and friendly, so if you want a lap cat, a Burmilla might be the right one for you.

Factastic:

The Burmilla appeared in its first cat show in 1983 and was recognised by Great Britain the same year. But US recognised the breed later in 1990.

Ancestry	Introduced in	Coat length	Coat Colour	Fur Type
Burmese and Chinchilla Persian	Great Britain in 1981	Short	Silver undercoat with chocolate tips	Fine, soft and thick

Lavender Persian

Introduction: Lavender Persians are one of the most recent groups added to the Persian category only in the 1960's.

Description: The desired colour for a Lavender Persian is a pinkish-dove-grey but it is very difficult to find the exact shade.

Behaviour: Persians aren't like most cats when it comes to being playful, but they are a pleasure to be with.

Factastic:
The Persian can have any of the three faces – the show quality, the breeder quality and the pet quality!

Ancestry	Introduced in	Coat length	Coat Colour	Fur Type
Angoras and Persians	1880's in Great Britain	Long	Pinking, dove-grey	Fine, thick and silky

Donskoy

Introduction: Irina Nemikina generated the Donskoy breed of hairless cat from hairless kittens abandoned by people thinking they had a disease.

Description: Donskoys come in four different types of coat, with various colours. They are elegant and sturdy and have a strong bone structure.

Behaviour: Intelligent, friendly, lovable and soft-hearted, the Donksoy doesn't like to live alone. It needs a companion. Ever heard of a pet for a pet?

Factastic:
Did you know that when the first Donskoy was born in 1987 in Elena Kovaleva's house, everyone thought that the cat had a disease and disowned it!

Ancestry	Introduced in	Coat length	Coat Colour	Fur Type
Unknown	Russia in 1987	Hairless	Various	None

Savannah

Introduction: Born to a Serval and a Siamese, the Savannah is a large-eared, medium-sized African cat.

Description: The Savannah is a wild-looking cat and the spotted pattern of the coat adds to this look. It is tall and lean with long legs and neck.

Behaviour: The Savannah only looks wild. In every way it is a domestic cat, friendly and affectionate. It is known to greet its owners with friendly head bumps.

Factastic:

The Savannah was named after the 'Savannahs' – the habitat of the Serval, one ancestor of the breed.

Ancestry	Introduced in	Coat length	Coat Colour	Fur Type
Serval and Siamese	USA in 1986	Short	Brown spotted	Fine

Chestnut Ticked Tabby Oriental shorthair

Introduction: This variety has hairs ticked chocolate on a bronze background. The tabby markings are chocolate too.

Description: Tickings are darkest on hair ends and tabby markings are restricted to the head, legs and tail.

Temperament: Orientals are very confident – they will hold firm even against bigger cats and dogs!

Factastic:

In Great Britain, this variety is popularly known as 'Chocolate'.

Ancestry	Introduced in	Coat length	Coat Colour	Fur Type
Siamese crosses	Great Britain in 1950's	Short	Blue	Fine and glossy

Chestnut Classic Tabby Oriental shorthair

Introduction: These cats have chocolate tabby markings on a bronze background. The classic 'M' on the forehead and the 'necklace' is defined.

Description: The bright green eyes of Chestnut Classic Tabbies are rimmed with chocolate!

Temperament: Orientals will sulk if left alone! Even at night, they would want to cuddle you in the bed rather than staying alone.

Factastic:

Orientals love heat – the hotter it is, the better!

Ancestry	Introduced in	Coat length	Coat Colour	Fur Type
Siamese crosses	Great Britain in 1950's	Short	Blue	Fine and glossy

Brown Tabby and White Norwegian Forest

Introduction: Norwegian Forests have a section in their ruff which they are known for, called their 'mutton chops' – but it has nothing to do with food!

Description: The brown tabby markings and the classic 'M' on the forehead are prominent. A bit of white on the nose adds to their beauty.

Behaviour: These cats are wonderful hunters – so if you have parrots, mice or other such pets, beware!

Factastic:
Norwegian Forests are believed to have travelled the world with the Vikings protecting their grain on land and sea.

Ancestry	Introduced in	Coat length	Coat Colour	Fur Type
Angoras and Shorthairs	Norway in 1520's	Semi-long	White with brown tabby markings	Woolly and glossy

Chocolate Lynx Point Siamese

Introduction: As with all dark-shaded Lynx point, the classic 'M' on the forehead can't be missed.

Description: The Chocolate Lynx Point has an ivory-coloured body marked with warm chocolate points which are broken with bands of white.

Behaviour: Siamese get bored very easily and should not be left alone for a very long time.

Factastic:
In Enid Blyton's *Bimbo and Topsy*, Bimbo is a Siamese cat.

Ancestry	Introduced in	Coat length	Coat Colour	Fur Type
Non-pedigree Asiatics	Thailand in 1300's	Short	White and chocolate	Fine and glossy

Seal-point Himalayan

Introduction: The Himalayan has a cobby body, rounded face, small ears, short strong legs and a short bushy tail.

Description: Seal-point Himalayans have a nice brown colouration but they do not have the same dark shade as the Seal-point Siamese because of the length of their coat.

Behaviour: Himalayans are friendly and playful and exhibit a tolerance level not found in many cats.

Factastic:
Himalayans like the luxuries of life! A nice comfortable bed and warm fire during the winter is a must!

Ancestry	Introduced in	Coat length	Coat Colour	Fur Type
Persian and Siamese	USA in 1920's	Long	White with seal brown colouration	Very fine, soft and thick

Black Smoke and White Maine Coon

Introduction: During the colder months, the Maine Coon's coat is very thick but during the hotter months, it loses most of its fur and looks like any other shorthaired cat.

Description: The Maine Coon is known for the ruff around its neck. This particular form has white ruff.

Behaviour: If curiosity ever killed a cat, it would be a Maine Coon! Maine Coons are very curious cats and love to poke their nose everywhere.

Factastic:
Unlike other cats, the Maine Coon is not averse to water. In fact, it is often seen playing with water dripping from taps!

Ancestry	Introduced in	Coat length	Coat Colour	Fur Type
Non-pedigree Persian	1770's in USA		White with black shading	Thick, silky and of uneven length

GLOSSARY

Adaptable: able to change or be changed in order to deal successfully with new situations..

Agile: able to move quickly and easily.

Agouti: light and dark banding of hair.

Amber: a yellowish brown colour.

Anatomical: related to the body of a cat .

Annihilate: to destroy something completely.

Bicolour: of two colours .

Bobbed: hair cut so that it hangs loosely to the level of the chin all around the back and sides.

Bran: the outer covering of grain which is left when grain is made into flour.

Breeder: a person who breeds cats.

Breeding: the producing of young cats.

Calico: American description for tortoiseshell and white.

Camouflage: the manner in which an animal's colour and shape matches its surroundings making it difficult to see .

Canned food: food preserved and packed in a can.

Carbohydrate: an energy rich food substance such as sugar or starch.

Carnivorous: meat eating animal.

Cat Fanciers' Association: the largest cat registry of the world.

Cat show: show primarily involving display of cats.

Catnip: a plant that cats love.

Chamois leather: leather made of hide of a small deer (called Chamois) living in mountains of Asia and Europe.

Champion: title accorded to a cat after a number of wins at cat shows.

Characteristic: a typical feature or quality.

Cobby: short and compact body.

Cross breeding: mating of two different breeds of cats.

Desert: area of land that has very little water and plants.

Dilution (colour): pale colour.

Domestic cat: a cat living with humans in their homes.

Down hairs: soft, short, secondary hair.

Dry food: Food that has very little moisture, usually sold in bags.

Energetic: having a lot of energy and enthusiasm.

Forests: large area of land thickly covered with trees.

Genes: contain encoded information (DNA) responsible for the characteristics of a breed.

Grease: thick oily substance.

Grooming: brushing done to keep the fur of a cat clean.

Guard hairs: longest hair forming the topcoat.

Habitat: place where a particular type of cat is normally found.

Hue: a particular shade of colour.

Lactating: a female cat producing milk to feed her kittens.

Litter: number of kittens reproduced by a cat.

Longy: cats with long tails but not a full-length tail.

Mackerel: a sea fish with greenish blue bands on its body.

Necklace: darker markings encircling the neck.

Non-pedigree: not from a line of pure breed cats.

Non-toxic: not poisonous.

Nutrition: food or nourishment.

Odd eyed: one eye different from the other.

Oriental: of the East.

Origin: starting point, source, ancestry.

Overcoat: warm outdoor coat.

Patch: large distinguishable area.

Pattern: regular or logical form.

Pedigree: recorded line of ancestry of pure breed cats.

People-oriented: preferring companionship of humans.

Points: tip or extreme end.

Polishing mitt: a hand glove for polishing.

Polydactyl: with more than five toes.

Predator: preying naturally on other animals.

Pregnant: having a young one developing in the uterus.

Protein: organic compounds composed of amino acids and forming an essential part of all living organisms.

Purebred: cats that have not been crossed with other breeds.

Query: question.

Recessive: appearing in offspring only when not masked by an inherited dominant characteristic.

Rosette: rose petal-shaped.

Ruff: coloured ring of hair around an animal's neck.

Rumpy: cat with no tail.

Self coloured: cats with one solid colour.

Slicker brush: brush used to take out dead hairs from a cat's fur.

Smoking: colouring pattern on a cat's fur.

Stumpy: cat with a tail as big as a stump.

Tabby: coat markings which are either spotted or ticked or blotched or a mix.

Taper: narrowing towards one end.

Temperament: behaviour.

Ticked: coloured at ends.

Torbie: tortoiseshell tabby.

Tortie: tortoiseshell.

Tortoiseshell: female cats showing black and other colours with distinct light and dark areas.

Undercoat: awn and down hairs.

Wedge shaped: shape of the head of certain cat breeds.

Wet food: canned food that has high moisture levels.

Whiskers: long facial hairs of a cat.

Breed List

American Bobtail
Auburn Turkish Van
Bengal Leopard
Black American Bombay
Black American Curl
Black and White American Curl
Black and White Norwegian Forest
Black and White Persian
Black and White Scottish Fold
Black and White Sphynx
Black British Shorthair
Black Exotic Shorthair
Black Maine Coon
Black Persian
Black Silver Abyssinian
Black Silver Mackerel Tabby European Shorthair
Black Smoke and White Cornish Rex
Black Smoke and White Maine Coon
Black Smoke and White Norwegian Forest
Black Smoke British Shorthair
Black Smoke Egyptian Mau
Black Smoke Persian
Black Turkish Angora
Black-tipped British Shorthair
Blue and White Cornish Rex
Blue and White Persian
Blue British Shorthair
Blue Burmese
Blue Cream Persian
Blue Korat
Blue Lynx Point Birman
Blue Lynx Point Siamese
Blue Mackerel Tabby Turkish Angora
Blue Mitted Ragdoll
Blue Oriental shorthair
Blue Persian
Blue Point Siamese
Blue Silver Somali
Blue Smoke Cornish Rex

Blue-cream and White Scottish Fold
Blue-eyed White British Shorthair
Blue-eyed White Persian
Blue-gray Chartreux
Blue-point Himalayan/Colourpoint Persian
British Longhair
Brown and Spotted White Siberian
Brown Classic Tabby Maine Coon
Brown Classic Tabby Persian
Brown Mackerel Tabby and White American Curl
Brown Tabby and White Maine Coon
Brown Tabby and White Norwegian Forest
Calico Persian
Calico Scottish Fold
Calico Van Persian
Calico White Cornish Rex
Champagne Burmese
Chausie
Chestnut Classic Tabby Oriental Shorthair
Chestnut Ricked Tabby Oriental Shorthair
Chinchilla Persian
Chocolate British Shorthair
Chocolate Lynx Point Siamese
Chocolate point Birman
Chocolate Silver Somali
Chocolate Tortie Persian
Chocolate-tipped Burmilla
Cinnamon Oriental Shorthair
Colourpoint shorthair
Colourpointed British Shorthair
Cream and White Persian
Cream British Shorthair
Cream Burmese
Cream Lynx Point Siamese
Cream Lynx Point Si-rex Devon Rex

Cream Persian

Cream Point Birman

Cream Turkish Van

Cymric

Dilute Calico Devon Rex

Diluted Calico Persian

Domestic Shorthair

Donskoy

Golden Persian

Golden-eyed White British Shorthair

Havana Brown

Honey Mink Tonkinese

Japanese Bobtail

Kurilian Bobtail

LaPerm

Lavender Persian

Lilac Point Siamese

Manx

Munchkin

Odd-eyed White Persian

Ojos Azules

Orange-eyed White Persian

Oriental Bicolour

Peterbald

Pixie-bob

Ragamuffin

Red and White Persian

Red Burmese

Red Classic Tabby British Shorthair

Red Mackerel Tabby British Shorthair

Red Oriental Shorthair

Red Persian

Red point Birman

Red Silver Mackerel Tabby European Shorthair

Red Smoke Cornish Rex

Red Tabby Persian

Ruddy Abyssinian

Ruddy Somali

Russian Shorthair

Savannah

Seal and White Point Snowshoe

Seal Bicolour Ragdoll

Seal Lynx Point American Curl

Seal Lynx Point Birman

Seal Point Ragdoll

Seal Point Siamese

Seal Tortie Lynx Point Birman

Seal Tortie Point Birman

Seal-point Himalayan/Colourpoint Persian

Selkirk Rex

Sepia Agouti Singapura

Serengeti

Serval

Shaded Silver Persian

Silver Classic Tabby American Shorthair

Silver Egyptian Mau

Silver Ocicat

Silver Tabby Maine Coon

Silver Torbie Devon Rex

Silver Torbie Exotic shorthair

Skookum

Sorrel Abyssinian

Sorrel Silver Somali

Sorrel Somali

Thai

Torbie Persian

Tortoiseshell Persian

Toyger

Turkish Vankedisi

White Angora

White Cornish Rex

White Maine Coon

White Oriental Shorthair

White Turkish Angora